Sonoma County...
its bounty

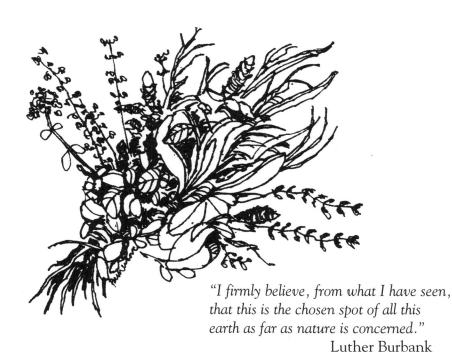

*"I firmly believe, from what I have seen,
that this is the chosen spot of all this
earth as far as nature is concerned."*
Luther Burbank

ISBN: 0-9658701-0-3

Published by
E. D. Moorehead
Petaluma, CA 94952

CREDITS

Ellen Moorehead, editor/coordinator
Orienne Bennett, recipe formatting
Don Bennett, copywriting and editing, co-sponsor pages
E. Ross Parkerson, art sketches
Hal Moorehead, expediting and accounting
Scott Hess, photography
Lynn Imm, design

Front cover credits: Scott Hess, photography; Lynn Imm, design; setting courtesy of Armida Winery; Sonoma County food products Fiesta Market. Back cover credits: Scott Hess, photography; Lynn Imm, design. Sonoma County scenes.

Printed in the USA by

WIMMER
The Wimmer Companies
Memphis

TABLE OF CONTENTS

Articles about "Sonoma County – Its Bounty" co-sponsors are located throughout the book. Without these essential Sonoma County restaurants, wineries and food producers, this cookbook would not have been possible.

PREFACE

Specialty cookbooks such as this can arise from a wide range of circumstances and situations. Organizations, groups, churches, even entire communities often get together to pool their culinary contributions.

This project, on the other hand, began with my love for cooking and eating good, healthy food, and my understanding that here, in Sonoma County, are some of the nation's most accomplished and innovative chefs.

As I began to explore ways to bring the combined expertise of these outstanding chefs to the world at large, I was led to a friend of all Northern California, Clover Stornetta Farms and its president, Dan Benedetti. With his vision, Dan expanded upon my ideas with a number of helpful suggestions. When the Board of Directors of Clover Stornetta Farms accepted the project, I then chose an editorial and art staff: Don Bennett and Orienne Bennett, artist E. Ross Parkerson, photographer Scott Hess, and designer Lynn Imm, all recognized for their skills and expertise and for whom we are ever thankful.

It has been a pleasure to work with everyone who has made this book possible. I know I have learned much and have gained new friendships. People who work with the earth and the food and wine thereof are special.

Read about them, visit them, and try their recipes. You will be thankful for these contributors, as are we, and grateful that the proceeds from this book will help non-profit organizations which are working to support sustainable agriculture.

Enjoy Sonoma County!

Ellen Moorehead,
Editor

FOREWORD

The following people are the owners of Clover Stornetta Farms. They have made this book possible:

Gene and Evelyn Benedetti, "Herm" and Marilyn Benedetti, Dan and Anne Benedetti, Gary and Lynn Imm, Kevin and Mary Imm, Mike and Dianne Keefer, John and Pat Markusen, and Paul and Lois Ross. All of us call Sonoma County "home."

We are personal friends of many of the participating restaurateurs, hotelieres, growers, and processors mentioned in the following pages. We thank all of you for your dedication and hard work and for being a part of this book.

We all share a love for our county. Together we have worked hard to sustain a healthy and nutritious food supply. Our commitment to excellence in every aspect of agriculture from field to table has vaulted Sonoma County to the top in food and wine appreciation nationally.

In our effort to support the future of quality agricultural production in Sonoma County, the owners of Clover Stornetta Farms, dedicate the proceeds of this book to Sonoma County Agricultural Fund c/o Sonoma County Community Foundation.

We invite you to share our pride.

Dante B. Benedetti, President
Clover Stornetta Farms, Inc.

ACKNOWLEDGMENTS

Whenever a project such as this book reaches completion, the editor recalls its inception and the people who helped to make it possible.

First of all, my appreciation and thanks go to Dan Benedetti, Gary Imm, Gene Benedetti, Herm Benedetti, and the family and Board of Directors of Clover Stornetta Farms, Inc., for giving support to this book and to me.

Clover Stornetta Farms not only has special products, it has special people who contribute to a warm and friendly atmosphere. I personally thank Betty Visser, Tami Dockery and Martha Kuhn, Clover Stornetta Farms employees, for their kindness and support.

Marcia McGlochlin, a friend for years and a member of the Clover staff, contributed knowledge and expertise and encouraged me, as did friends Marcie Becker and Leroy Lounibos.

Lynn Imm not only gave her design talent on the cover, but gave of herself to keep me "on track." Patti Baker contributed her culinary talent by checking recipes and giving help to me when, at times, the "going seemed a little rough."

My appreciation goes to the Culinary Committee who chose the chefs/restaurants, and to Chef Charles Saunders, who gave much of his time and his talent to guide me with this cookbook. Two young men he trained, Brian O'Neal and Nat Tate, have also been a great help.

Thank you Randy Hankins, Lyndi Brown, Carol Kozlowski-Every, Ruth Waltenspiel, Mike Pendergast, Tom Wark, Trevor Lawrence, Tim Fish, Michele Anna Jordan, Peggy Biltz, Nancy Fletcher, Chef Klaus E. Scheftner, Jeff Cox, Sandra Verteegh, John Fisher and Bruce and Steve Cousins.

Thank you, Wimmer, for Karen Clements, Sheila Thomas and Kay Molpus, without whose help the cookbook wouldn't exist, and thank you Anne and Willis Rivinus of our former home, Bucks County, Pennsylvania, who helped us in the beginning with information and an introduction to Wimmer.

Ellen Moorehead, editor

THE BOUNTY OF SONOMA COUNTY

"I firmly believe, from what I have seen, that this is the chosen spot of all this earth as far as Nature is concerned." Luther Burbank, discussing Sonoma County.

Ask almost anyone who lives here, and they'll tell you Sonoma County is one of the world's finest places to live.

Sonoma County has beauty, variety, a temperate climate, some of the world's finest wines, a rich history, and agricultural abundance and diversity.

About beauty – Sonoma County has a magnificent Pacific coastline, priceless towering redwood groves, mountains, and emerald green hills in mid-winter.

About the climate – Sonoma County, because it seldom drops below freezing in the winter, boasts green hills in January, and summers cooled by the ocean fog. This distinctly Mediterranean climate contributes to the high quality of Sonoma County's ag products.

About diversity – the County's southern region boasts dairies, the western region produces some of America's most sought-after seafood, and much of the County features world-class vineyards. The Sebastopol area is home to the famed Gravenstein apple, truck farms growing produce for the Bay Area's finest restaurants are everywhere, and finest-quality poultry and lamb are also found throughout the County. Small organic vegetable farms and greenhouses now provide produce daily to the area's finest restaurants. A range of micro-climates enables Sonoma County to produce not just a wide variety of outstanding wine grapes, but also other sought-after agricultural products.

About fine wines – Sonoma County has major wine regions which produce outstanding varietal wines, with more than a hundred wineries open to the public.

About history – Although first visited by England's Sir Francis Drake, Sonoma County was the point where the imperial expansion of Russia and Spain met in the early 1800s. The Sonoma Mission was founded by the Spanish to counter Russia, which had a settlement at Fort Ross. Then, the Sonoma settlement was the site of the famed Bear Flag Revolt, where American settlers declared their independence from Mexico and set in motion a chain of events that led to California's annexation by the United States.

Because of all of the above, Sonoma County is a popular destination for 7.1 million visitors a year. Foremost among them are movie makers, who have been using the geographical backdrops and quaint settings for movies since days of the silents. Alfred Hitchcock chose Santa Rosa for Shadow of a Doubt because of its all-American qualities; George Lucas chose Petaluma for American Graffiti (as did Francis Ford Coppola for Peggy Sue Got Married) for its evocation of nostalgia. Hitchcock returned to Bodega and Bodega Bay for his classic, The Birds. Along the way, hundreds of other movie and TV directors and commercial producers have used Sonoma County settings.

Perhaps Sonoma County's greatest visitor attraction, however, is its food. Because so much high quality produce, poultry, seafood, and meat is grown here for San Francisco's finest restaurants, it was inevitable that the county would develop its own restaurants to rival the best the big city had to offer. Throughout Sonoma County, from the cities to the smallest villages, excellent restaurant choices are available.

In this book, we have gone to these outstanding chefs and asked them to share their know-how in converting the "bounty of Sonoma County" into truly memorable feasts.

THE CLOVER STORNETTA STORY

Clover Stornetta Farms traces its beginnings to the early 1900s, when most of the area dairy ranchers formed Petaluma Cooperative Creamery to distribute their dairy products under the Clover label. In those first years, milk and butter were shipped daily down the Petaluma River to San Francisco.

Clo the Clover Cow, the humorous mascot for Clover Stornetta Farms, Inc., has symbolized Sonoma County's dairy industry for almost three decades, having made her debut in 1969.

Clo and her pun-filled billboards (outstanding in her field, tip Clo through your two lips, mooing pitcher star, Supreme Quart) have tickled motorists for years. Clo has also become a fixture in local parades, events, and public appearances. Behind Clo are the family dairies that make up the region's dairy industry.

Also behind Clo is a concentrated effort to place Clover Stornetta Farms at the forefront of the movement towards organic and sustainable dairying in the State of California. Clover took the lead last year with the announcement of the North Coast Excellence-Certified (NCE) program. Clover Stornetta has a contractual agreement with local producers stipulating that dairies will not use the bovine growth hormone rBST. In addition, herds supplying milk to Clover Stornetta Farms are required to maintain high standards of dairy cleanliness and herd care. NCE milk consistently far surpasses all state and federal standards.

In 1975, the biggest fire in Petaluma history destroyed the cooperative's processing and bottling operations, and the board of directors sold the wholesale distribution arm of the business to several employees, who are today's owners. That sale included the Clover brand and Clo.

Originally operating from several locations, Clover Stornetta consolidated all its operations in Petaluma in 1991. With a new, fully automated and computerized plant, Clover can now do three times the volume of their old plant with the same manpower.

Today, as it was in the early 1900's, family farming is still the backbone of North Coast dairying, a way of life for hundreds of ranchers committed to providing high quality milk to Bay Area consumers. Clover Stornetta Farms Inc. is proud to be a leader, working with these dedicated producers to deliver the healthiest milk products possible. Clover Stornetta has also received recognition for its extensive humanitarian and charitable involvement in the North Bay area.

For more information regarding Clover Stornetta Farms:
91 Lakeville Street - P.O. Box 750369
Petaluma, CA 94975-0369
707-778-8448
FAX 707-778-0509

Miss Sonoma Cownty

At Clo's range

APPETIZERS

MARINATED PORTOBELLO MUSHROOMS

Petaluma Mushroom Farm, Inc., Chef Todd Fisher

This appetizer tastes like filet mignon rather than mushrooms.

1 pound Portobello
   mushrooms
Salt

Freshly ground white pepper
Extra virgin olive oil

Season the mushrooms with salt, white pepper and extra virgin olive oil to taste and grill over heat 4 minutes until soft. Let cool. Marinate 1 hour in mixture below; chill before serving.

MARINADE:

3 ounces extra virgin olive oil
1 teaspoon chopped fresh parsley
1 sprig fresh rosemary,
   chopped

1 small shallot, chopped
1 clove garlic minced
2 limes, juice only

Serves 2-3 people as an appetizer

WARM CARAMELIZED PEARS WITH PROSCIUTTO

Katie Wetzel Murphy, Alexander Valley Vineyards

2 ripe large pears
3 tablespoons butter
½ teaspoon sugar
8 thin slices prosciutto

Mint sprigs
Fresh ground black pepper
Balsamic vinegar, boiled and
   reduced to half volume.

Heat butter and sugar, add pears and cook, turning gently until pears are lightly caramelized. Depending on ripeness of pears, cooking will vary; they should be tender, but not too soft. Add water as needed, deglazing until pears are done and covered with a light caramel syrup. Place pears on plate, slice and drape with prosciutto. Grind a little fresh black pepper over pears. Place a drop of Balsamic vinegar reduction between each slice of pear. Garnish with mint sprig. Serve with AVV Chenin Blanc.

4 servings.

NAPOLEON OF EGGPLANT, TOMATO, BASIL AND FRESH MOZZARELLA OR GOAT CHEESE ON A BED OF SONOMA COUNTY GREENS

Klaus E. Scheftner, Chef Klaus Catering

For each appetizer serving you will need the following:

1 thick (½ inch to ¾ inch) slice of peeled eggplant approximately 3 inches across, brushed with garlic and olive oil. Grill and then marinate with a dusting of Italian herbs, very little salt, ground pepper and a few drops of lemon juice.

1 whole Roma tomato sliced in ⅛ inch oval discs
Fresh basil leaves
Sliced fresh Mozzarella discs or goat cheese
A small amount of Sonoma County greens to include some frisee and possibly arugula

On a 7" or 8" plate, make a bed of greens. Center a slice of eggplant and arrange tomatoes and basil, alternating in a circular fashion. Top with slices of cheese and crown with sprig of basil. Add fresh ground pepper and drizzle with a balsamic vinaigrette (made with best quality olive oil).

ROAST GARLIC

Phillip Breitweiser, Chef, "The Cafe" Sonoma Mission Inn

5 pounds garlic, peeled   8 ounces olive oil

Mix garlic and oil into a roasting pan. Cover with foil and bake at 350 degrees for approximately one hour.

100 servings.

VIANSA SMOKED SALMON BITES WITH CAPER-ONION MASCARPONE

Vicki Sebastiani, Viansa Winery

This recipe could also be served on cucumber slices. Simply substitute ¼ inch thick slices of cucumber for the baguette slices.

¼ cup capers, minced
¼ cup minced white onion
1 teaspoon minced lemon zest
¼ cup mascarpone cheese
   (cream cheese can be
   substituted)

1 tablespoon sour cream
½ sourdough baguette, sliced
   into 16 slices, ¼ inch thick
8 ounces smoked salmon
   (16 slices)
32 leaves Italian parsley

In a food processor or blender, purée capers, onions, lemon zest, mascarpone and sour cream. Cut baguette slices in half and spread each half with one teaspoon of the caper mixture. Top with piece of smoked salmon, rolling or folding over if necessary. For garnish, dab a tiny spot of caper mixture on the bottom of each parsley leaf and "glue" to the top of the salmon slice.

32 servings

VELLA'S CHEESE PUFFS

Sally Vella, Vella Cheese Company

These golden-brown puffs, which resemble cookies, are mouth watering appetizers or accompaniments for soup or salad (they also freeze well). They are another favorite of the Vella Family.

2½ tablespoons butter
3½ tablespoons flour
Pinch salt
 Cayenne to taste

5 tablespoons grated Dry Jack
   cheese
3 egg whites, stiffly beaten

Preheat the oven to 400 degrees. Melt the butter over medium heat and blend in the four with a whisk. Remove the pan from the heat and blend in the salt, cayenne and grated dry jack. Fold in the egg whites. Drop the batter from the tip of a small spoon onto a buttered cookie sheet, leaving one inch between spoonfuls. Bake until toasty brown, 12 to 15 minutes.

Makes about 15 puffs.

ROSEMARY FLATBREAD WITH CARAMELIZED ONIONS, GOAT CHEESE AND KALAMATA OLIVES

Gerald Lowe, Bear Flag Cafe

Can be cut into small pieces for hors d'oeuvres or larger pieces for a main course with a salad.

FLATBREAD DOUGH:

½ tablespoons dry yeast
½ tablespoons sugar
¾ cup tepid water (110 degrees)
¼ cup olive oil

1 teaspoon salt
½ teaspoon rosemary, finely chopped
3-4 cups all-purpose flour

Mix together yeast, sugar and water in stainless bowl and let stand 10 minutes. Add 1 cup of the flour and the oil, salt and rosemary. Stir and add enough of the flour to form a dough Knead dough 10 minutes adding flour to form a smooth dough. Place in a large bowl and cover with plastic and allow to proof about one hour.

TOPPING:

1 large yellow onion, sliced thinly
15 Kalamata olives, pitted and halved

½ pound dry Sonoma Jack cheese, grated
½ pound goat cheese

Preheat oven to 425 degrees. While the dough is rising prepare the filling. Peel and slice onion and sauté in large pan with 1 tablespoon olive oil. Cook slowly until onions turn golden and caramelize. Allow to cool. Punch down dough and roll out in a rectangle about ¼ to ⅛ inch thick and transfer to a half sheet tray or a jelly roll pan about 8 x 16 inches. Spread Sonoma Jack cheese evenly over flatbread. Spread onions evenly over the cheese. Crumble goat cheese into small pieces and spread evenly over the onions. Spread olives over onions. Bake 10 to 15 minutes until golden brown.

MUSSELS STEAMED IN KENDALL-JACKSON CABERNET SAUVIGNON WITH BASIL, GARLIC AND LEMON

Chef Brian Leonard, La Crema Winery

This is my fat-free take on Moules Mariniere, the traditional Provençal dish which uses butter and white wine for steaming mussels. I prefer cooking the mussels in Cabernet Sauvignon, as it adds a more complex dimension to the strongly flavored seafood. This recipe easily can be doubled to serve more people.

1½ cups Kendall-Jackson Cabernet Sauvignon
4 cloves garlic, peeled and sliced
3 stems fresh basil with leaves
3 green onions, cut into 2 inch pieces
1 medium tomato, seeded and chopped
½ lemon, sliced crosswise into rounds
½ tablespoon freshly ground black pepper
1 pound fresh mussels

Wash and scrub the mussels under cold running water. With a knife, carefully scrape off the beard (grassy threads) attached to the shells. Set aside. Heat the Cabernet Sauvignon in a large, heavy saucepan over high heat. Add the garlic, basil, onions, lemon and black pepper and bring the mixture to a boil. Add the mussels to the pot, cover and steam over medium-high heat just until the mussels are fully opened, about 3 to 5 minutes, stirring occasionally. Discard any mussels which do not open fully. Serve the mussels and their cooking liquid in soup bowls with hot French bread for dipping into the sauce, or spoon over steamed rice.

Yield: Makes 4 appetizer servings or 2 main course servings

PESTO AND CALIFORNIA DRY MONTEREY JACK CHEESE TOPPING OR DIP

California Milk Advisory Board

Combine 1 cup fresh California lowfat plain yogurt, or sour cream, with ¼ cup prepared pesto. Add ¼ cup finely grated California Dry Monterey Jack cheese, and season with salt and pepper to taste.

Makes about 1⅓ cups, 5 servings, about ¼ cup each

FRESH TOMATO AND BASIL (OR TARRAGON) TOPPING OR DIP

California Milk Advisory Board

1 large tomato
1 cup fresh California lowfat plain yogurt, lowfat cottage cheese, or sour cream

¼ cup chopped fresh basil (or 2 tablespoons chopped fresh tarragon)
½ teaspoon salt
¼ teaspoon freshly ground pepper

Peel tomato, cut in half then scrape out and discard seeds. Chop the tomato finely and combine with plain yogurt, cottage cheese, or sour cream, basil (or tarragon), salt and freshly ground pepper.

Makes about 1½ cups; 6 servings, about ¼ cup each

BASIL AND ROASTED RED PEPPER TOPPING OR DIP

California Milk Advisory Board

1 cup fresh California sour cream, lowfat plain yogurt, or lowfat cottage cheese
⅓ cup chopped, roasted, peeled, red peppers

¼ cup chopped fresh basil
¼ teaspoon salt
¼ teaspoon freshly ground black pepper

Combine sour cream, lowfat plain yogurt, or lowfat cottage cheese, with red peppers, basil, salt and freshly ground pepper.

Makes about 1⅓ cups; 5 servings, about ¼ cup each.

VEGETABLE DIP

National Dairy Council

An excellent dip for crisp vegetables, or dressing for a spinach salad or sauce for fish.

1 large cucumber, peeled, seeded and diced
1 cup plain yogurt

Salt, pepper and fresh herbs to taste

Combine all ingredients.

AVOCADO DIP

National Dairy Council

Serve as a dip with tortilla chips or topping for tacos, enchiladas or hamburgers.

½ cup plain yogurt
1 ripe avocado, mashed

¼ cup diced tomato
Chili powder to taste

Combine all ingredients.

LEMON CHIVE TOPPING OR DIP

California Milk Advisory Board

1 cup fresh California lowfat plain yogurt, lowfat cottage cheese or sour cream
3 tablespoons chopped fresh chives
1 tablespoon fresh lemon juice
½ teaspoon finely grated lemon zest
¼ teaspoon salt
¼ teaspoon freshly ground pepper

Into yogurt, lowfat cottage cheese, or sour cream, stir chives, lemon juice, lemon zest, salt and freshly ground pepper.

Makes about 1 cup; 4 servings, about ¼ cup each.

JASMINE BOULETTES
WITH FONTINA CHEESE

Lisa Hemenway

Serve as a side dish with grilled chicken or fish. It is also a great appetizer served with your favorite dipping sauce.

2 cups Jasmine rice
4 cups water
¾ teaspoons salt

Cook rice as directed and cool. Then mix with the following ingredients:

½ cup sliced green onions
¾ tablespoon mustard seeds, toasted
½ cup grated Fontina cheese
2 eggs
Bread crumbs (add to bind if mixture is not sticky enough to ball)
1 teaspoon chopped fresh basil
Salt and black pepper

Scoop into 2 ounce balls and compress densely. Roll balls in bread crumbs. Deep fry until golden grown.

Yield: 24 boulettes

BOREGO SPRINGS BUTTERMILK BREAD

Dairy Council of California

This versatile bread tastes like "More, please." It goes especially well with scrambled eggs or perhaps a cheese omelet for brunch or luncheon. Good, too, with meat and seafood salads. It is a perfect snacktime treat when spread with butter or cream cheese. When cut into finger or bite-size pieces, it becomes a canapé of distinction.

1½ cups buttermilk
1 egg
3 cups biscuit mix
2 tablespoons sugar
1 cup (about ¼ pound) grated
   Swiss cheese

1 cup sliced pimento stuffed
   olives, drained
¾ cup chopped walnuts,
   optional

Combine buttermilk, egg, biscuit mix and sugar; beat one minute to blend thoroughly. Gently stir in Swiss cheese, olives and walnuts. Spoon into well-buttered loaf pan, (9 x 5 x 3 inch or comparable size). Bake in a 350 degree oven for 50 to 55 minutes. (A crack along the top of the loaf usually occurs.) Cool five minutes before removing from pan. Continue cooling on wire rack. Unused portion will keep well when wrapped and stored in refrigerator or freezer.

SAGANAKI

Engel Recipes, Topolos' Russian River Vineyards and Restaurant

The following recipe is from the forthcoming cookbook A La Grecque by Bob Engel and Christine Topolos, published by Full Circle Press.

8 ounces Kasseri cheese, grated
1 teaspoon red wine vinegar
1 teaspoon lemon juice

½ teaspoon Greek oregano
1½ tablespoon Metaxa or
brandy

Use a heavy skillet, cast iron or aluminum, of about 6 or 8 inches in diameter. Melt the cheese slowly over medium low heat, stirring occasionally. When mostly melted raise the flame to high, stir in the red wine vinegar and lemon juice, sprinkle the top with the oregano. Have a match ready! Pour the brandy around the outer edge and ignite. Hoopa! Serve with crusty bread.

This is a rough and sizzling fondue, not smooth and creamy like the French version. It is flamed with Metaxa or brandy at the table, starting any meal off with a flourish. Very good with Zinfandel or Pinot Noir.

VELLA'S CHEESE CAKES

Vella Cheese Company

These cheese cakes are wonderful appetizers. Great with salad or soup. They freeze well.

2½ tablespoons butter
3½ tablespoons flour
Pinch of salt
Cayenne pepper to taste

5 tablespoons grated Dry Jack
cheese
3 egg whites

Preheat oven to 400 degrees. Melt butter under medium heat. Add flour and blend with a whisk. Stir until well blended. Remove from heat. Add salt, Cayenne pepper and grated Dry Jack and blend. Fold in stiffly beaten egg whiles. Drop the mixture from the tip of a small spoon onto a buttered cookie sheet one inch apart. Bake 12-15 minutes. Remove when "toasty brown."

CHELSEA'S CHEESE CHIPS

Linda Viviani, Sonoma Cheese Factory

These can be stored in plastic bags in the refrigerator for several weeks. It is much healthier taking this snack to the movies or serving them before dinner.

Semi hard cheeses such as   Garlic Jack, Hot Pepper
  traditional Sonoma Jack,   Jack, Sonoma Cheddar

Cube cheese. On a Teflon baking sheet, place each cube of cheese 3 inches apart and bake for 8 to 10 minutes at 375 degrees. The longer you bake, the more the butterfat melts away and the crisper the chip.

ABOUT FILO

Engel Recipes, Topolos' Russian River Vineyards and Restaurant

The following recipe is from the forthcoming cookbook A La Grecque by Bob Engel and Christine Topolos published by Full Circle Press

A one-pound package of filo contains about 20 individual leaves. You will find filo in the frozen foods section of most supermarkets. Follow the directions for thawing the filo given on the box. If the dough tears into strips or crumbles as you fold it, it has probably been mistreated in storage: dropped, thawed and re-frozen, or otherwise abused. Return it and try a market that might have a higher turnover or take more care with their product.

Many cooks seem intimidated by filo, which is unnecessary. The instructions on the box may warn you to work quickly and keep the dough covered with a damp cloth, but this should be required only on very hot, dry days. if you have your materials assembled and work at a steady pace you should have no trouble.

Unused portions of the dough can be re-frozen, but be very certain to wrap well. Use a plastic freezer bag and seal with freezer tape. Obviously filo which was in poor condition when frozen will not profit from the experience. Save only soft pliable dough.

TIROPITAS - FILO CHEESE TRIANGLES

Engel Recipes, Topolos' Russian River Vineyards and Restaurant

The following recipe is from the forthcoming cookbook A La Grecque by Bob Engel and Christine Topolos published by Full Circle Press.

½ pound feta cheese	2 teaspoons minced parsley
¾ cup cottage cheese	1 dash each of nutmeg and
1½ tablespoon grated Kasseri	white pepper
or Parmesan cheese	1 package filo dough
1 egg, beaten lightly	½ pound butter, melted

Place cheeses, egg, parsley, nutmeg and pepper in a bowl and stir with a spoon or fork. Don't mash the bits of feta to a smooth paste. Stir just enough to combine. The luncheon size uses a full sheet of filo folded in thirds.

For the appetizer tiropita, first cut the whole package of filo in thirds. These long strips of filo for the smaller presentation need only be folded in half. Work with one packet at a time. Wrap the extras to protect them from drying out.

Brush a sheet of filo lightly with butter, then fold it in thirds. The technique for folding the triangles is the same, a simple "flag fold". The larger tiropita will require a rounded tablespoon of filling; the smaller one just a teaspoon. Brush each strip with butter and fold up. Place on a lightly oiled sheet pan and brush the tops with butter. Bake the hors d'oeuvres size at 375 degrees for 12 to 14 minutes, the large sized ones for 15 to 20 minutes. The tops should be just golden, not browned deeply. Never microwave filo.

Uncooked tiropitas keep very well. Store in the refrigerator for several days or up to a month in the freezer. Thaw only a few minutes, then bake immediately. Do not store once thawed. These precautions will prevent filo getting soggy before it has a chance to bake.

These classic Greek cheese pastries can be made in either appetizer or luncheon size. Three of the luncheon sized triangles make a nice meal. Allow about the same number of the cocktail size per person for hors d'oeuvres.

Yield: 20 luncheon sized, 70 or more appetizers

TZATZIKI

Engel Recipes, Topolos' Russian River Vineyards and Restaurant

The following recipe is from the forthcoming cookbook A La Grecque by Bob Engel and Christine Topolos.

2 medium cucumbers	2 teaspoons minced garlic
2 cups plain yogurt	1-2 dashes of white pepper

Peel the cucumber and cut in half the long way. Use the tip of a spoon to scoop and scrape the seeds out. Discard the seeds. What you end up with looks like a pair of dugout canoes. Grate the cucumber or use a food processor to chop it very finely. Put the grated or chopped cucumber in a sieve and squeeze vigorously to remove all water. You could also put the cucumber in a towel and wring the juice out. If you want to make a very thick yogurt such as they have in Greece, line a sieve with cheesecloth, set in a bowl and drain the yogurt overnight in the refrigerator. In Greece they use a pillowcase (and often skip the refrigeration!) Combine the cucumber meat, yogurt and garlic in a bowl. Add white pepper and more garlic to taste.

This simple dip for bread is very low in salt and fat and makes an excellent alternative to butter.

Yield: 2½ cups

ARMADILLO EGGS

TEXAS STYLE STUFFED HARD COOKED EGGS
Nu-Cal Foods, Inc.

12 large fresh eggs	½ cup cream cheese
6 fresh jalapeño peppers, minced	¼ cup dry bread crumbs

Hard cook the eggs. Cool and shell, then cut in half. Mash yellows with minced jalapeños, cream cheese and bread crumbs. Stuff back into whites and refrigerate until ready to serve.

Yield: 24 halves

SMOKED SALMON STUFFED EGGS

Nu-Cal Foods, Inc.

12 large fresh eggs
⅓ cup sour cream
1 tablespoon grated onion
2 teaspoons finely chopped
    fresh dill

8 drops Tabasco sauce
4 ounces smoked salmon,
    chopped
24 tiny dill sprigs

Hard cook the eggs. Cool and shell, then cut in half to make 24 shells. Mash yellows and mix with cream, onion, chopped dill, Tabasco sauce and salmon. Spoon yellow mixture back into shells. Garnish with dill sprigs.

Yield: 24 halves

PEAR-BRIE QUESADILLAS

Carol Shelton, Windsor Vineyards

This easy appetizer can be done on the grill, while it's heating up, if you're having an outdoor party.

6 soft flour tortillas, 6 inches
    in diameter
3 ripe Bartlett pears
1 tablespoon fresh lemon juice

1 bunch cilantro or basil,
    shredded
1 small wheel Brie or
    Camembert cheese,
    medium ripe

Slice pears thinly and sprinkle with fresh lemon juice. Cut cheese into ¼ inch slices. Place one tortilla in a 6-8 inch sauté pan over medium-low heat. When it feels a bit warm, lay overlapping slices of pear, cilantro and Brie on it and top with another tortilla. Heat another 30 seconds or so, then cut in wedges and serve, garnished with a "fan" of thinly sliced pear and a cilantro sprig.

Yield: Serves 6

POLYNESIAN BEEF BITES

Shoffeitt Seasonings

This dish can be served over rice or as an appetizer.

1½ pounds ground beef
¾ cup quick oats
1 5 ounce can water chestnuts,
   drained and sliced

1 teaspoon Shoffeitt Lemon
   Teriyaki Seasoner
1 egg
½ cup milk

Mix all ingredients well and form into small balls and brown on all sides, or bake on a cookie sheet (drain off fat).

SAUCE:
1 8½ ounce can crushed
   pineapple
½ cup vinegar
1 cup packed brown sugar
2 tablespoons corn starch

1 cup beef bouillon
⅓ cup chopped bell peppers
2 teaspoons Shoffeitt Lemon
   Teriyaki Seasoner

Drain pineapple (save juice), mix sugar, corn starch and add juice, bouillon, vinegar and Lemon Teriyaki. Bring to boil, cook until thick and clear. Stir in bell peppers and pineapple. Add sauce to meat balls.

TORTA LAYERED WITH SUN-DRIED TOMATO, PESTO, PINE NUTS AND CREAM CHEESE

Christine Motarex, for Paradise Ridge Winery

1 6 inch tart shell
16 ounces cream cheese
 (2 packages)
½ cup sweet butter (1 stick)
1 cup sun-dried tomatoes
 (1 small jar)

1 cup pine nuts
1 cup basil
1 clove garlic
1 tablespoon lemon juice

Purée sun-dried tomatoes, place into a strainer and drain off any oil. Set aside

Toast pine nuts on a dry skillet until golden brown. Finely chop or grind in a food processor. Press pine nuts into bottom of a 6 inch tart shell. Set aside.

Blend basil, lemon juice, garlic, ½ stick butter and 1 package cream cheese until smooth. Carefully spread pesto onto pine nuts with a wet spatula. Be careful not to mix pine nuts into pesto. Place in refrigerator and chill until set (about 20 minutes).

Whip remaining ½ stick of butter and 1 package of cream cheese together. Spread this layer on top of pesto layer. Refrigerate until cold and set (about 1 hour).

Spread sun-dried tomato purée on the top of the cream cheese, cover with plastic and keep refrigerated until ready to serve. Serve with crackers or sliced baguette.

Variation: Use half parsley and half cilantro instead of basil. You can also add roasted garlic to the plain cream cheese layer.

12 or more

PERUVIAN POTATOES
(PAPAS A LA HUANCAINA)

Patricia Salmon, Bodega Goat Cheese

This is a wonderful appetizer or main meal accessory.

Cook 6 to 8 red boiling potatoes until just tender. Peel. Slice. Arrange a bed of red leaf lettuce on a serving platter. Arrange potato slices on top.

SAUCE:

½ teaspoon turmeric
1 jalapeño peppers
10-12 crackers
2 cloves fresh garlic
1 tablespoon olive oil

1 8 ounce container (½ pound) of jalapeño or plain goat cheese
Milk to thin to preferred consistency
Salt and pepper

Blend ingredients in a blender. Pour sauce over potatoes. Garnish with olives, sweet red peppers or sliced hard boiled eggs. Serve at room temperature.

8 servings

MUSHROOMS A LA GLORIA

Gloria Ferrer

6 tablespoons butter, room temperature
1 tablespoon minced garlic
1½ pounds mushrooms, cleaned, stemmed

1½ cups Gloria Ferrer Brut sparkling wine
Salt and pepper to taste
1-2 tablespoons minced fresh parsley or mixed fresh herbs

In a 10 inch skillet, melt 3 tablespoons of the butter over medium heat, add garlic. Cook and stir garlic until lightly browned, add mushrooms. Cook, stirring occasionally, until lightly browned, about 5 minutes. Add Gloria Ferrer Brut, bring to boil. Reduce heat, simmer until liquid is reduced to ⅓ cup, about 10 minutes. Taste and adjust seasoning with salt and pepper. Remove from heat. Whisk in remaining butter until sauce is slightly thickened. Arrange mushrooms in serving dish with toothpick inserted in each. Pour sauce over. Garnish with minced parsley or fresh herbs.

Yield: Serves 6

OLIVE TAPENADE

Michele Anna Jordan

2 cups Kalamata olives
1½ cups Niçoise olives
6 garlic cloves, peeled and
    minced
1 tablespoon Italian parsley

2 anchovy fillets, packed
    in oil, rinsed
⅓ cup extra virgin olive oil
Black pepper in mill

Remove the olive pits and discard them. Using a very sharp knife, mince the olives (do not use a food processor). Place them in a small mixing bowl, and toss with the garlic and parsley. Using a small mortar and pestle, pound the anchovies until they form a paste. Add the paste to the olives, pour in the olive oil, and toss together lightly. Let sit 30 minutes before using.

About 2 cups

©1997 Michele Anna Jordan, recipe appears in California Home Cooking (Harvard Common Press, 1997)

CROSTINI WITH GOAT CHEESE
AND MUSHROOMS

Twisted Vines

Toast or grill thinly sliced baguette that has been spread with garlic butter. Cover toast with a layer of goat cheese and sautéed mushroom mix. Heat through in a 400 degree oven for about 5 minutes.

MUSHROOM MIXTURE:
4 cups each slice Portabellos
    and shiitakes (regular mush-
    rooms can be substituted)

Unsalted butter
½ cup minced shallots

Sauté mushrooms in butter with the shallots until mushrooms are done. Salt to taste.

Proportions may vary depending on the amount of servings desired.

J GREEN GARLIC AND FENNEL AIOLI

Chef Thomas Oden, Jordan Winery

For garlic lovers! Add a dollop of this fresh mayonnaise to raw oysters and enjoy with a glass of J, a great combination of "sparkling" creaminess.

2 egg yolks, room temperature
¼ cup J, Jordan Sparkling
   Wine
3 fresh green garlic, white part
   only (or garlic cloves), very
   finely chopped

2 tablespoons finely chopped
   fennel leaves
Salt and white pepper to taste
¾ cup light olive oil
¼ cup extra virgin olive oil

Whisk together the egg yolks, salt, pepper, fennel leaves and the J in a double boiler over simmering water. When the mixture just begins to thicken, remove it from the heat, and start adding the light olive oil, a few drops at a time, until an emulsion begins to form between the egg mixture and the oil. Start adding the oil in a thin stream as you continually whisk, until all of the oil is incorporated. Add the extra virgin olive oil in the same manner until it is also incorporated into the emulsion, which should be of the consistency of mayonnaise with a glossy sheen. Serve with oysters on the half shell.

Yield: Enough for 4 dozen oysters

J MIGNONETTE

Chef Thomas Oden, Jordan Winery

2 shallots, finely chopped
4 tablespoons J, Jordan
   Sparkling Wine
2 teaspoons dill vinegar

Fresh dill to taste, finely
   chopped
Freshly ground black pepper
   to taste

Mix all of the ingredients together. Serve on the side with oysters on the half shell.

Yield: Enough for 24 oysters.

FOCACCIA ALLA CARLO

Kenwood Vineyards and Winery

1 pound flour
1 teaspoon salt
1 cup lukewarm water
1 cake yeast

2 tablespoons olive oil
2 cups Salsicce Alla Vin Zin
 Sauce (recipe follows)
½ cup grated Asiago cheese

Dissolve yeast in lukewarm water. Place sifted flour and salt on board; add dissolved yeast. Knead thoroughly for 15 minutes. Add oil; continue kneading until smooth ball is obtained. Cover well. Set aside in warm place about 3 hours or until dough has raised to double its size. In the meantime, prepare Salsicce Alla Vin Zin Sauce (recipe below). When dough has raised, spread in large well-greased baking pan about ½ to ¾ inches thick. Dent here and there with finger tips. Pour generous layer of sauce over dough; sprinkle liberally with grated cheese. Bake in hot oven for ½ hour. Lower heat; continue baking for 15 minutes or to a golden brown.

SALSICCE ALLA VIN ZIN SAUCE:

¼ cup best quality olive oil
6 Italian sausages
6 large garlic cloves, chopped
1 medium onion, chopped
2 8 ounce cans tomatoes,
 undrained
1 5½ ounce can tomato paste
2 teaspoons dried oregano

2 teaspoons dried basil
1 6 inch cinnamon stick
 (broken in half)
¼ teaspoon hot red pepper
 flakes
Salt and freshly ground black
 pepper to taste
½ cup Kenwood Vineyard
 Sonoma Valley Zinfandel

Heat oil in large saucepan. Add sausages and fry until browned, about 10 minutes. Drain and set aside. In the same pan add garlic and onion and cook until onions are tender, about 4 minutes. Add tomatoes, tomato paste, oregano, basil, cinnamon stick, pepper flakes, salt, pepper and Zinfandel. Lower heat and simmer for about 30 or 40 minutes. Add sausage and simmer for another 1 to 3 hours stirring occasionally.

This sauce may also be served over hot pasta. You can pass grated parmesan cheese and a pepper mill to your guests if they want to add to the taste.

J POLENTA AND
WILD MUSHROOM POPOVERS

Chef Thomas Oden, Jordan Winery

Hearty, fragrant and warming. Popovers with an Italian twist that can stand alone or accompany your favorite veal recipe...great with J.

FILLING:

½ pound wild mushrooms, cut in bite-size pieces (save the small and broken ones, chopped fine, for the sauce)

2 tablespoons butter
2 tablespoons oil
1 medium garlic clove, minced
2 tablespoons chopped parsley

Trim the ends of the mushrooms and clean them with a small brush. Heat the butter and oil in a sauté pan. Add the garlic and mushrooms and cook over medium heat for several minutes or until tender. At the last minute, toss with parsley. Set aside.

BATTER:

½ cup polenta, cooked according to package directions
2 ounces butter
½ cup milk

2 eggs, well beaten
1 teaspoon salt
½ cup flour
1 tablespoon baking powder

Add the butter and the milk to the cooked polenta. Mix, then add the eggs. Sift together the dry ingredients and add them to the mixture. If necessary, add more milk to thin to a heavy batter consistency.

SAUCE:

1 cup J, Jordan Sparkling Wine
1 shallot, finely chopped
2 tablespoons heavy cream
½ teaspoon chopped fresh thyme

Salt and white pepper to taste
Finely chopped wild mushroom pieces
½ pound firm sweet butter, cut into small dice

Reduce the J and the shallots to ¼ cup. Add the cream, thyme, mushrooms, salt and pepper and bring to a boil. Simmer for 5 minutes, reduce the heat to low, and whisk in the butter rapidly. Allow to sit over a pilot light until ready to serve.

FOR APPETIZERS (FOR 4)

Preheat a muffin pan in a 450 degree oven. Remove from the oven and brush the cups (4 of them) with butter, and fill halfway with the polenta batter. Add a tablespoon of mushrooms and cover with more polenta. Bake for 20 minutes, reduce the temperature to 325 degrees and bake to 10 to 20 minutes longer or until done. Serve with the mushroom beurre blanc, and garnish with shaved Parmesan.

FOR HORS D'OEUVRES (FOR 10)

Follow above directions with mini muffin pans (2 ounce capacity), or drop one tablespoon of the polenta batter on a buttered, preheated cookie sheet. With a small spoon, make a well in the polenta to accommodate one teaspoon of the mushroom sauté. Cover with another tablespoon of polenta. Bake in a preheated 425 degree oven for 5 minutes, or until risen, then lower the heat to 300 degrees for about 10 minutes more. Garnish with grated Parmesan cheese and chopped parsley.

BAKED PORTOBELLO AND SONOMA GOAT CHEESE WITH BASIL TOMATO CONCASSÉ

Kenwood Restaurant and Bar, Proprietor Chef Max Schacher

4 5 inch Portobello mushroom caps
4 slices of Sonoma goat cheese
4 medium diced tomatoes, peeled and seeded

2 tablespoons chopped shallots
1 tablespoon chopped garlic
2 tablespoons olive oil
4 branches of basil

Remove stems from Portobello mushrooms, place on a baking sheet with one slice of goat cheese on each. Bake for 20 minutes in a 350 degree oven. In a medium sauce pan place oil, shallots, garlic, diced tomatoes, salt and pepper to taste. Cook for ten minutes.

To serve: Cover bottom of hot plate with concassé. Center Portobello on the concassé. Garnish with basil.

4 servings.

SONOMA CHEESE FACTORY
SONOMA, CALIFORNIA

SONOMA CHEESE FACTORY

The famed SONOMA JACK BRAND is a moist, semi-soft, rindless cheese, produced by the family at the plant and store located in Sonoma's historic Plaza. It was founded in 1931 by Celso Viviani, who traced his roots to the 11th century in Lucca, Italy. After arriving in the U.S., Celso worked for a local winery until Prohibition, when he began work producing cheese at the Sonoma Mission Creamery. Today, the business is run by his son Pete and grandson David.

Jack cheese, created by David Jacks in 1882 in Monterey, is California's first indigenous cheese, Teleme being the second. The Vivianis produce many different flavors of Sonoma Jack, from garlic to Habañero, the hottest of the pepper cheeses. They also produce ricotta, Teleme, and Sonoma Cheddar.

You are invited to visit the Sonoma Cheese Factory to sample premium, award-winning Real California Cheeses, explore the wine department and the sumptuous gourmet food section, and enjoy the vine-covered hillsides.

As David Viviani says, "if the grape's leap to immortality is wine, then milk's leap to immortality has to be cheese." The Sonoma Cheese Factory welcomes you to experience the unique and immortal gastronomic pleasures of Sonoma Valley.

2 Spain Street, On the Plaza
Sonoma, CA 95476
797-996-1000 or 1-800-367-1947
FAX 707-935-3535

Center City Diner

Enter Center City Diner, Petaluma's only new age Eatery. Center City serves retro dinner classics and new American fare in keeping with the bounty that is Sonoma – featuring fresh baked breads, creative entrees and great desserts. Come in and experience the difference.

107 Petaluma Blvd. No.
Petaluma, CA 94952
707-766-9232

J. Pedroncelli Winery

offers wines that are flavorful, accessible, consistent and affordable. Pedroncelli wines are rich with varietal and fruit and subtle complexity, beautifully balanced and ready to enjoy on release. "Our wines reflect the region's outstanding grapes," says John Pedroncelli. "We use gentle methods to bring out softness and age in small oak barrels to gain complexity." Pedroncelli has added two special lines – Single Vineyard Selection and Primavera Mista and Primo Misto proprietary blends.

1220 Canyon Road
Geyersville, CA 95441

KORBEL CHAMPAGNE CELLARS

We invite you to visit our historic winery here in Sonoma County's Russian River Valley, where we have been producing fine méthode champenoise California champagne for over 100 years.

Just north of Santa Rosa, off Highway 101, take the River Road exit and drive west approximately 14 miles. Tours, tasting and retail sales daily.

**13250 River Road
Guerneville, CA 95446
(707) 887-2294**

F. Korbel and Bros., Inc.

Timber Crest Farms

Just out Dry Creek road, past the grapevines and before you reach the lake, you'll find our Timber Crest Farm. It sits on a little knoll in Sonoma County – about an hour and a half north of San Francisco and 15 miles from the Pacific Ocean.

For more than 40 years, our family has farmed this fertile land. Together, we've planted, grown, harvested, dried and packaged our unsulphured dried fruits, nuts, and dried tomatoes. And if we have learned one thing, it's to add nothing – no additives and no attitude. As Ron and I like to say, the only thing we add to what we package is pride. Our Sonoma Brand foods are now available nationwide.

When you are in this area, please stop by for a tour. During the summer months we can show your our foods from ground to table. Enjoy.

Ruth and Ron Waltenspiel
4791 Dry Creek Road
Healdsburg, CA 95448
707-433-8251

SOUPS

AUTUMN SQUASH SOUP

Chef Sarah Deane, Korbel Champagne Cellars

1 large butternut squash
2 large yellow onions
2 large yams
5 cups chicken broth
½ cup soy sauce

1 cup orange juice
1 cup Korbel Blanc de Blanc
  Champagne
2 cloves garlic

Preheat oven to 350 degrees. Bake yams and butternut squash for one hour. Let cool enough to handle and remove skins. Set pulp aside. Pour champagne into a large soup pot. Peel and chop onions into large dice and add with garlic to champagne. Simmer over medium heat 10 minutes then add pulp and chicken broth. Continue to cook 20 more minutes. Add soy sauce and orange juice. Remove from heat and let cool enough to purée in a food processor until smooth. Return to heat to warm before serving. For variations you can add curry powder, ginger or sour cream.

4-6 servings

WILD MUSHROOM SOUP

Michael Valmassoi, Center City Diner

1 tablespoon cepes, dry
Brandy to cover
½ large onion, chopped
½ teaspoon chopped garlic
6 cups chicken stock or
   vegetable stock
1¼ pound domestic
   mushrooms, chopped

4 ounces Chanterelle
   mushrooms, chopped
¼ bottle dry white wine
4 cups cream
Nutmeg
Lemon juice

Soak cepes in brandy, then wok off alcohol, about 5 minutes. Strain through fine chinoise and save brandy. Clean cepes and chop. Sweat onions and both mushrooms with garlic in large pot. Add brandy and white wine. Reduce by ⅔. Add stock. Reduce by ⅓. Add cream and season with salt, pepper, nutmeg and lemon juice to taste.

4-6 servings

RED PEPPER AIOLI

Chef Sarah Deane, Korbel Champagne Cellars

1 jar roasted red pepper
2 egg yolks
1 whole egg (both at room
   temperature)

1 cup safflower oil
1 teaspoon lemon juice
½ teaspoon salt

In a food processor purée red peppers with yolks and egg. Pouring with the motor still on, slowly drizzle oil into mixture to thicken. Add in lemon juice and salt. Use for garnishing soup.

CARROT AND BASIL SOUP
WITH ORANGES

De Loach Vineyards

½ cup (4 ounces) unsalted
   butter
6-8 carrots, peeled and chopped
3 celery ribs, chopped
1 onion, chopped
2 large navel oranges, pith,
   membrane and peel
   removed, chopped

6 cups vegetable broth
¾ cups fresh basil leaves, stems
   removed
4 tablespoons orange crème
   fraîche (or sour cream
   mixed with fresh orange
   juice)

Pulse vegetables in batches in a food processor until they are coarsely chopped. Melt half the butter in a saucepan over moderately high heat and sauté vegetables until they begin to soften, about 5 minutes. Turn heat to high, add orange sections and vegetable broth and bring to a rolling boil. Lower heat and simmer for 45-50 minutes or until vegetables are very tender. Stir in butter and basil leaves. Purée soup in a blender in small batches until smooth. Season to taste with salt and freshly ground pepper. Strain soup into a large saucepan and heat through. Garnish with orange crème fraîche, sprigs of basil and thin strips of orange zest. Serve with De Loach Vineyards Russian River Chardonnay.

Serves 6 to 8

SHRIMP BISQUE WITH THAI CURRY YOGURT GARNISH

Chef Brian Leonard, La Crema Winery

This is a low-fat alternative to a traditional bisque, as it uses the reserved shrimp shells for both flavoring and as a thickening agent instead of the usual cream and butter, very much like the French Sauce l'Americain which uses lobster shell. Don't worry though...the soup is strained and the shells are discarded instead of eaten! I think you'll find this a wonderfully light soup, well suited as either a starter to an elegant meal or ample light dinner when accompanied with salad and hot fresh bread.

1 pound large (18-count) shrimp
1 tablespoon plus 1 teaspoon olive oil
3 stalks celery, trimmed and diced
2 medium carrots, peeled and diced
1 medium yellow onion, peeled and diced
1 large potato, peeled and diced
2 large cloves garlic, peeled and crushed

2 medium tomatoes, seeded and diced
1 cup La Crema Chardonnay
4 cups chicken or vegetable stock
1 teaspoon fresh thyme
½ teaspoon salt
1 pinch cayenne pepper
½ cup plain non-fat yogurt
1 teaspoon green or yellow Thai curry paste
1 tablespoon minced fresh cilantro leaves for garnish

Peel the shrimp, reserving the shells, and set aside. Heat 1 tablespoon oil in a large, heavy saucepan over medium-high heat. Add the celery, carrots, onion and potato and sauté over medium-high heat until limp, about 5 minutes. Add the garlic and shrimp shells and sauté for an additional 2 minutes. Add the wine and cook over high heat until reduced by half, about 5 minutes. Add the tomatoes, stock, salt, cayenne and thyme. Lower heat and simmer for 25 minutes. Meanwhile, place the yogurt and curry paste in a small bowl and whisk together until well blended. Set aside. In three batches, process the soup in a food processor blender. Strain the mixture through a fine sieve into a clean pot, pressing against the solids with the back of a spoon to extract as much liquid as possible. Place the pot over medium-low heat to warm the soup. Heat the remaining oil in a small sauté pan over medium-high heat. Add the shrimp, season with salt and pepper to taste, and sauté until pink, about 2 to 3 minutes. Spoon the soup into 6 bowls and top with a dollop of the Thai Curry Yogurt. If desired, drag the tip of a sharp knife through the yogurt, making a decorative pattern in the soup. Divide the sautéed shrimp among the soup bowls and garnish each portion with minced cilantro leaves. Serve immediately.

Yield: 6 servings (6 cups)

VICHYSSOISE WITH SONOMA CHEDDAR

Linda Viviani, Sonoma Cheese Factory

½ cup chopped onions
4 cups diced raw potatoes
2 leeks, cubed
2 cups chicken stock
1½ cups sharp Sonoma
   Cheddar Cheese, crumbled

½ cup sour cream
½ teaspoon celery salt
½ cup fume blanc white wine
Chives, minced
dash cayenne pepper

Combine potatoes, leeks, onions, chicken stock and bring to a boil. Cook until potatoes are tender. Combine all ingredients in blender and blend until smooth. Chill overnight. Serve with sprinkling of minced chives and a dash of cayenne.

4-6 servings

ROCK SHRIMP BISQUE

James D'Ottavio, Cafe Buon Gusto

2 tablespoons olive oil and
   unsalted butter
1 cup sliced mushrooms
1 cup sliced onion
½ cup sliced celery
2 teaspoons crushed garlic
2 teaspoons dry thyme
Salt and pepper
1 cup dry white wine

1 cup clam juice
4 ounces unsalted butter
1 cup flour
3 cups milk
1 cup tomato sauce (canned
   or your own marinara style
   sauce)
1 cup shelled rock shrimp
1 cup light or heavy cream

Sauté mushrooms, onion, celery, garlic, thyme, salt and pepper
in olive oil and butter. Deglaze with wine and reduce to ½. In
sauce pan (8 cup) combine unsalted butter melted with flour to
make roux. Add milk slowly to roux to desired creamy thick
consistency. Add sautéed vegetables and tomato sauce. Blend
with hand blender or in food processor. Return to heat and add
shelled rock shrimp and cream, bring to boil then allow to
simmer for 5-10 minutes. Adjust seasonings to your taste.
A warm and satisfying meal in itself.

4-6 servings

CHILLED CUCUMBER SOUP

Christian Bertrand, Glen Ellen Inn Restaurant

5 cucumbers, chopped
1 red onion, chopped
½ cup rice vinegar
2 teaspoons salt
1 teaspoon white pepper

4 teaspoons chili powder
¼ cup dill, chopped
1 cup water
2 cups sour cream

Combine all ingredients; purée. Chill in refrigerator for at least
2 hours. Serve in chilled soup bowls, garnish with fresh dill springs.

Serves 6.

Dempsey's Alehouse. - Petaluma

Pachman '96

CHILLED SONOMA TOMATO-VEGETABLE SOUP

Executive Chef, Martin Courtland, Chateau Souverain

16 ripe tomatoes, blanched, peeled and seeded
4 English cucumbers, peeled and seeded
4 red bell peppers, peeled and seeded
2 celery stalks
½ medium onion
1 jalapeño pepper, cored, seeded and chopped fine
1 serrano chile, cored, seeded and chopped fine
8 ounces tomato juice
2 ounces Sherry wine vinegar
3 ounces olive oil
¼ cup chopped mixed herbs (Italian parsley, chives, cilantro and tarragon)
Salt, freshly ground pepper and cayenne pepper to taste.

After vegetables have been peeled, cored and seeded, cut everything into 1 inch pieces. Place them in a stainless steel bowl along with the jalapeño pepper and serrano chile. Add the vinegar, tomato juice and olive oil. Season lightly with salt, freshly ground pepper and cayenne pepper. Cover tightly and refrigerate overnight, stirring occasionally. Place mixture in a food processor and, using the pulse setting, mince until the vegetables are fine but still have some texture to them. Return mixture to bowl and add the freshly chopped herbs, and correct the seasoning (to taste). Chill well and serve in ice cold bowls.

12 servings

USES FOR YOGURT IN SOUPS

National Dairy Council

Top borscht, gazpacho or cream of tomato soup with dollop of plain yogurt and minced chives.

Windsor Vineyard

is America's original direct wine merchant, established in 1959. For ten years, Windsor Vineyards has been America's number one award-winning winery, earning 1,751 awards. Winemaker Carol Shelton was recently awarded the Andre Tchelistcheff Award for winemaking excellence by *Bon Appetit* magazine. Our vineyard designated wines and premium varietals are sold exclusively through mail order and telemarketing and allow a special message or logo to be printed on each bottle. Call for free catalog.

P.O. Box 368
Windsor, CA 95492
800-333-9987

Chateau Souverain

is a striking Sonoma County architectural landmark whose wines are made from each variety's best growing region: Cabernet Sauvignon, Merlot and Sauvignon Blanc from the Alexander Valley, Chardonnay and Pinot Noir from the Carneros and Russian River regions, and Zinfandel from Dry Creek Valley. Tasting room hours 10-5 daily, and the Café at the Winery featuring Chef Martin Courtman's cuisine is open Fri.-Sun. for lunch and dinner.

Independence Lane at Highway 101
Geyserville, CA
707-433-8281

The Glen Ellen Inn Restaurant

captures the spirit of the wine country with innovative, elegant California cuisine and an exciting Sonoma Valley wine list. With proprietor/chef Christian Bernard and his wife Karen, the Inn is the perfect place for those who are as passionate about food as well as life. The restaurant is well known among locals for unforgettable meals and gracious hospitality. Voted Sonoma County's Best Restaurant by the *Press Democrat*. Open nightly 5:30–closing.

13670 Arnold Drive
Glen Ellen, CA
707-996-6409

Paradise Ridge Winery

is an elegant wine estate dedicated to producing the finest estate grown Sauvignon Blanc, Chardonnay and sparkling wines. Nestled high on a hill in Santa Rosa's Fountaingrove area, the winery offers breathtaking views from the Santa Rosa plain to the Russian River Valley and beyond.

Paradise Ridge welcomes visitors for tasting and sales of their award-winning wines daily from 11 a.m. to 6 p.m. Wines by the glass are offered Wednesday evenings to enjoy while watching the sunset. Occasionally the winery is closed for special events.

Situated on a 156-acre estate of vineyards, wooded hillsides and meadows, the winery offers a private setting for special events, functions and weddings for up to 250.

4545 Thomas Lake Harris Drive
Santa Rosa, CA 95403
707-528-9463

Nu Cal Foods. Inc.

From the turn of the century until the 1950's, Petaluma, California, was indeed the egg capital of the world. Although many of the small egg producers are now gone from the Petaluma countryside, Nu Cal Foods, Inc. continues the proud tradition that made Petaluma a household name worldwide.

Our original farms were founded back in 1915. In those days, we had a mere 2,000 chickens. Today, we are still owned and operated by the same families that founded us. And, we still operate out of our original location in the rolling hills of Petaluma.

But, a few things have changed. Now we have more than a half million chickens on our farms, and we deliver more than 500,000 eggs to businesses throughout Northern California every day. Even so, our commitment to quality remains unchanged, and our primary goal is still the same as it was more than seven decades ago – to keep our hens happy, our eggs healthy, and our customers satisfied.

795 Liberty Road
Petaluma, CA 94952
707-795-8937

SALADS

INSALATA DI MOZZARELLA CON SALSA CRUDA

Chef Michael Ghilarducci, The Depot Hotel Restaurant and
Italian Garden

4 medium ripe tomatoes,
  peeled and seeded
2 teaspoons vinegar
1 tablespoon fresh chives,
  chopped
3-4 very tender inside celery
  stalks, finely diced
½ cup extra virgin olive oil

Salt
Pepper
12 ounces fresh mozzarella
  cheese, made with buffalo
  milk if possible
20 fresh basil leaves, washed
  and dried

Combine tomatoes, vinegar, chives, celery, olive oil, salt and
pepper in a food processor and purée well. Portion out this sauce
onto four individual serving plates. Slice the cheese and arrange
on the plates, allowing three nice slices per person. Garnish
each plate around the edge with three of the nicest basil leaves,
using 12 in all. Julienne the other 8 leaves and sprinkle this on
top of the cheese on each plate.

Serves 4

PASTA SALAD

Shoffeitt Seasonings

3 cups corkscrew macaroni
  (Rotini)
⅓ cup red bell pepper, diced
3 hard boiled eggs
1 cup mayonnaise
1 teaspoon sugar

Few drops of milk
3 stalks celery, sliced
½ cup diced onion
Shoffeitt Lemon Dill
1 cap full vinegar
½ teaspoon mustard

Cook macaroni as directed being careful not to over cook. Drain
and rinse with cold water. Add pasta to bowl and sprinkle generously
with Lemon Dill. Add celery, bell pepper, onion and gently mix.
Set aside. In a small bowl add mayonnaise, mustard, vinegar,
sugar and a few drops of milk. Mix until smooth. Add to macaroni
mixture and gently toss. Dice hard boiled eggs and add to salad,
tossing gently. Refrigerate at least 2 or 3 hours before serving.

THREE CHEESE TORTELLINI SALAD WITH PARSLEY VINAIGRETTE

Lynn Silva, Food for Thought

2 quarts cooked triple cheese
  tortellini
1 large red bell pepper
1 medium yellow bell pepper

1 medium red onion
1 12-ounce can artichoke
  hearts (in water)

DRESSING:
½ cup olive oil
⅓ cup red wine vinegar
3-4 garlic cloves, finely
  chopped

1 bunch parsley, finely
  chopped
1 teaspoon salt
¾ teaspoon black pepper
1½ teaspoon Italian seasoning

Slice all of the above vegetables in long thin strips. Add these to the tortellini in a large mixing bowl. Mix the dressing ingredients in a separate bowl and pour over the tortellini mixture. Chill and serve.

FAVA BEAN SALAD (SOLTERO, FROM CUSCO, PERU)

Patty Salmon, Bodega Goat Cheese

½ pound Queso Fresco
2 cups raw, fresh, young fava
  beans or raw peas (removed
  from pod and peeled from
  seed cover)
2 cups cooked corn

2 medium sized potatoes
  (cooked and chopped
  small)
1 red pepper (cut into skinny
  slivers)
1 large carrot (grated)
1 Bermuda onion (sliced thin)

Mix ingredients in a bowl. Arrange on a bed of lettuce.

DRESSING:
¼ cup salad oil
  Juice from 1 lemon or lime

Salt, cayenne pepper and
  pepper to taste.

Mix ingredients. Pour over salad just before serving.

8 servings

GREEK POTATO SALAD WITH DRIED TOMATOES

Timber Crest Farms

1 pound (3 medium) potatoes, uniform in size, sliced ¼ inch thick
1 cup (1½ ounces) dried tomato halves, cut in half (use kitchen shears)

Lemon Dressing, recipe follows
1 cup sliced seedless cucumber
½ cup sliced red onion
1 cup (4 ounces) feta cheese
½ cup Greek olives or pitted black olives

In a 2 to 3 quart saucepan, cook potatoes, covered, in 2 inches of boiling water 10 to 15 minutes, just until tender. Drain and cool. Meanwhile, in a bowl, cover dried tomatoes with boiling water; set aside at least 10 minutes. In a large bowl, prepare Lemon Dressing. Thoroughly drain tomatoes and pat dry with paper towel. Add potatoes, cucumbers and tomatoes to dressing and toss to coat. Mound mixture on a plate. Arrange onion, cheeses and olives on top.

LEMON DRESSING:
Whisk ¼ cup each olive oil and water, 2½ tablespoons lemon juice, 1 large clove garlic (pressed), 1 tablespoon chopped fresh oregano or 1 teaspoon dried, 1 teaspoon salt and ½ teaspoon pepper.

4 servings

MIXED GREEN SALAD WITH HONEY MUSTARD DRESSING

Chef Sarah Deane, Korbel Champagne Cellars

Whisk together 4 teaspoons of Dijon mustard with 4 teaspoons of honey. Toss with mixed greens and garnish with diced fresh pears and gorgonzola cheese. Optional; sprinkle with candied walnuts or pecans.

GREEK SALAD

Engel Recipes, Topolos' Russian River Vineyards and
Restaurant

The following recipe is from the forthcoming cookbook *A La
Grecque* by Bob Engel and Christine Topolos.

1¾ cups Greek olive oil	1 teaspoon salt
½ cup red wine vinegar	1 pinch each of dill, thyme
1 tablespoon Greek oregano	and mint

Whisk all together in a bowl or shake to blend in a jar.

Assemble the salad in layers with tomatoes and cucumbers on
the bottom, then the feta, red onions and parsley in that order.
Garnish with olives and Greek pepperoncini. Drizzle the dressing generously over the top just before serving. There should be
dressing to spare to dip bread in.

*A true Greek salad contains no lettuce. The base is wedges of tomato
and sliced cucumber, accented by crumbled feta cheese, thinly sliced
red onion, parsley and Calamata olives. But all these are nothing if
the dressing isn't just right. The recipe above is a surprisingly simple
one that will only be as good as the ingredients used. A good Greek
olive oil, slightly green and fruity, real Greek oregano, and a strong
varietal red wine vinegar are essential.*

Makes 2¼ cups

PAN GRILLED SIRLOIN SALAD IN BLACK PEPPER DRESSING

Cline Cellars

This is a delicious salad, with a strong influence of black pepper, is a perfect companion for the 1994 Syrah.

SIRLOIN SALAD:

1½ pounds New York sirloin
 Salt and ground black pepper

2 teaspoons olive oil
2 heads romaine lettuce

Season the steak with salt and pepper. Meanwhile, heat the olive oil in a sauté pan over high heat until smoking. Sear the steak on both sides of 3 to 4 minutes per side. Set aside.

BLACK PEPPER DRESSING:

¼ cup balsamic vinegar
¼ cup 1994 Cline Marsanne
2 shallots, chopped
2 cloves garlic, chopped
½ cup extra virgin olive oil

2 teaspoons cracked black
 pepper
⅓ cup grated Parmesan cheese
Salt to taste

Combine the vinegar, wine, garlic and shallots in a bowl. Whisk in the olive oil and add the pepper and Parmesan, mixing thoroughly. To serve, tear the washed and dried romaine leaves into large bowl, tossing with approximately ½ cup of the dressing. Divide the lettuce among 6 plates. Slice the steak thinly and arrange in a fan pattern on top of the lettuce. Drizzle the additional dressing over each plate.

Richard's Home and Sarabee's Vineyard – Windsor

Pakkum '96

SONOMA SUMMER SALAD
WITH GRILLED TUNA

Martin Courtman, Executive Chef, Chateau Souverain

Please read all instructions first.

MARINADE:

4 tuna steaks, 5 ounces each (approximately 1 inch thick)
2 teaspoons anchovy purée
2 teaspoons chopped fresh tarragon
2 teaspoons chopped Italian parsley
2 tablespoons chopped shallots
1 tablespoon fresh lime juice
1 cup olive oil
½ teaspoon Tabasco sauce

Mix together all ingredients. Place the tuna steaks in the marinade and chill in the refrigerator for one hour prior to grilling.

FOR THE SALAD:

8-12 ounces of spring mix (depending on the desired size of the salad)
½ small cucumber, peeled, seeded and cubed
24 sugar snap peas, blanched
2 hard boiled eggs, cut into fourths
4 roma tomatoes, peeled and cut into fourths
1 avocado, peeled and sliced
12 black olives
4 ounces grain mustard vinaigrette (may vary to your preference)

Tossing the salad: In a large bowl place the spring mix, snap peas, cucumbers and vinaigrette. Season with salt and freshly ground pepper, continue to toss the salad lightly until well mixed. Divide evenly onto four plates and add the egg, tomato, avocado and olive.

GRAIN MUSTARD VINAIGRETTE:

12 ounces Chateau Souverain Chardonnay (reduce slowly to 4 ounces)	2 cups canola oil
2 teaspoons whole grain mustard	1 teaspoon chopped fresh tarragon
	1 teaspoon shallots
	Salt and pepper to taste

Place the 4 ounces of reduced Chardonnay in a blender with the mustard. Blend on slow for 30 seconds and then add the oil very slowly. Once emulsified, and all the oil has been added, turn off the blender and place into a small bowl. Add the shallots and tarragon. Season with salt and freshly ground pepper. Refrigerate unused vinaigrette for up to one week. Shake or place in blender as it separates.

2½ cups

THE FINAL PRODUCT:

When ready to serve the Sonoma Summer Salad, it is important that everything is timed right. As soon as the tuna has marinated for about one hour, remove each steak and place on hot grill. For a medium-rare finish, grill tuna for 3 to 4 minutes on each side. Season with salt and freshly ground pepper just before placing on the freshly tossed salad. Serve immediately sprinkled with edible flower petals for a beautiful touch.

1 serving per tuna steak

INFUSED HERB OIL

Chef Sarah Deane, Korbel Champagne Cellars

Blanch parsley in boiling water. Refresh in ice water. Drain and dry. Add equal amounts of oil as herbs. Mix in blender to form a paste. Place in a clean jar and add three times as much oil as paste. Store one day and filter.

ROASTED PORK LOIN SALAD

Stuffed with Caramelized Fennel, Red Onion and Watercress,
Served with an Orange and Pink Peppercorn Vinaigrette

Jeffrey Madura, John Ash and Company

ROASTED PORK:

6 6 ounce tenderloins
1 medium fennel bulb, cored
  and cut into ¼ inch dice
1 medium red onion cut into
  ¼ inch dice
2 bunches watercress leaves,
  washed and picked and cut
  in julienne strips

3 tablespoon clarified butter or
  olive oil
Ground black pepper to taste
Kosher salt to taste
¼ cup olive oil

After cleaning and trimming pork tenderloins, place sharpening
steel into center of tenderloin and create a pocket for stuffing.
In a large sauté pan, heat clarified butter until hot. Add diced
fennel and red onion and coat well with butter. Caramelize the
onion mixture at high flame for 8 to 12 minutes. Once caramelized, cool mixture down. Once cooled, add watercress and
season with salt and pepper, mix well. Then take mixture and
stuff ¼ cup of each mixture into the pork tenderloin cavity.
Once all are stuffed, marinate in olive oil and salt and pepper
until ready to cook. Heat sauté pan with olive oil or heat grill
and cook pork tenderloins until medium, about 8 to 10 minutes.
Once cooked, let stand to retain juices and heat. While tenderloin sits, make salad and dressing.

SALAD:

2 medium fennel bulbs, thinly
  sliced vertically in ¹⁄₁₆ inch
  slices
2 medium red onions, thinly
  sliced in rings and shocked
  in water for 10 minutes.

2 bunches watercress,
  stemmed and cleaned
Kosher salt and ground black
  pepper to taste
2 blood or navel oranges,
  peeled and sliced into thin
  rounds ¼ inch thick

Arrange salad by mixing shaved fennel, red onion and watercress in stainless steel bowl Add kosher salt and ground black
pepper to taste and arrange attractively on 6 large platters. Then
add orange rounds to each bunch to give height. Cut tenderloin
into 6 pieces and arrange next to salad mixture. Drizzle with

orange and pink peppercorn vinaigrette (recipe to follow) and garnish with fennel frond.

ORANGE AND PINK PEPPERCORN VINAIGRETTE:

6 ounces unsweetened frozen orange juice concentrate
⅓ cup low sodium soy sauce
¼ cup rice wine vinegar
1 tablespoon peeled and minced fresh ginger
1½ teaspoon dark sesame oil

½ cup scallions, white and pale green parts
½ cup chopped fresh Italian flat leaf parsley
1 cup olive or peanut oil
¼ cup dry toasted pink peppercorns

In a food processor or blender, combine all ingredients except the oil and pink peppercorns. Process until smooth. Transfer to a bowl. Stir in the oil and peppercorns being careful not to emulsify, otherwise the dressing will be too thick. Store any unused dressing, covered and refrigerated, for up to two weeks.

Yield: Serves 6

GLEN ELLEN FIRE AND ICE SALAD

Christian Bertrand, Glen Ellen Inn Restaurant

FRESH FRUIT SALSA:

2 apples, diced
2 pears, diced
½ jalapeño, diced very fine
¼ cup diced red onions
Salt
Pepper

⅛ cup lemon juice
⅛ cup red wine vinegar
¼ cup fresh mint, chopped
½ bunch fresh cilantro, chopped

SALAD:

1½ cup sweet pecans
¾ cup sugar

1 pound mixed greens
2 ounces goat cheese, grated

Heat sugar over low heat until it turns to a caramel colored liquid; spread pecans on cookie sheet and drizzle caramel over top. Let cool. Chop pecans in fourths. Toss together all ingredients for the fresh fruit salsa; let marinate for six hours. Place mixed greens on chilled salad plate; top with fruit salsa, a healthy sprinkling of goat cheese and a handful of sweet pecans.

Serves 10.

SONOMA CHEESE AND CHICKEN SALAD WITH MIXED GREENS

SERVED WITH WALNUT DILL VINAIGRETTE
Sonoma Cheese Factory

2 large chicken breasts, halved
1 cup Sonoma Jack Cheese, shredded
1 medium red bell pepper, finely chopped
2 tablespoons chopped scallions
2 tablespoons butter
2 tablespoons cooking oil

Salt and pepper to taste
2 cloves garlic
8 cups mixed greens, including arugula, chicory, endive, raddichio
1 cup roasted walnuts, halved (put nuts on cookie sheet in 400 degree oven until slightly brown, about 10 minutes)

WALNUT DILL VINAIGRETTE:
2 cloves garlic
1 tablespoon Dijon mustard
¼ cup rice vinegar
¼ cup walnut oil
½ cup good quality salad oil

1 inch fresh peeled ginger
1 teaspoon dill weed
Salt and pepper to taste
½ teaspoon sugar

Heat oven to 350 degrees. Cut a pocket in each chicken breast with a sharp knife, working horizontally from the thickest part of the breast down. Stuff each breast with a mixture of the cheese, pepper and scallion. Sauté garlic cloves in oil/butter until golden and remove. Brown chicken breasts on each side on medium high heat and then bake in oven for 20 to 25 minutes until cooked. Let cool. Cut on diagonal into 8 ribbon slices. Divide greens onto 4 plates. Using spatula, lift chicken ribbons and place on greens. Drizzle vinaigrette over each plate and garnish with walnuts.

Yield: Serves 4

WARMED RED CABBAGE SALAD WITH GOAT CHEESE AND BACON

Jeffrey Madura, John Ash and Company

1 pound smoked bacon or
    pancetta (good quality)
1 teaspoon peeled and minced
    garlic
½ cup fruity olive oil
2 tablespoons wild honey
⅓ cup red wine vinegar
½ teaspoon each salt and
    freshly ground black pepper

1 pound red cabbage, cored
    and finely shredded
5 ounces capriccio or chabis
    goat cheese
Baby frisée and mache or
    watercress and nasturtium
    flowers for garnish

Cook bacon until lightly browned and just crisp. Roughly chop and set aside. Reserve ¼ cup of the bacon fat and combine in a bowl with the garlic, olive oil, honey, vinegar, salt and pepper. Taste and correct seasoning. In a large sauté pan over moderate high heat, briefly warm the olive oil mixture, add the cabbage and toss quickly for a minute or two just to warm through. Add chopped bacon and place on warm plates garnished with frisée, mache and nasturtium flowers. Thinly slice goat cheese and arrange attractively on top.

Serves 6 to 8

ROUILLE

Chef Sarah Deane, Korbel Champagne Cellars

1 egg yolk
Roasted garlic
Dijon mustard

Olive oil
Salt and white pepper

Combine yolk, garlic and Dijon in a food processor. Drizzle in olive oil. Paprika to color.

KENDALL-JACKSON

HEALTHY CUISINE –
IT'S ALL ABOUT FLAVOR

by Brian Leonard
Chef, Kendall-Jackson Winery

One of the pleasures, one of the necessities, and with a spreading waist dawning, one of the curses of being a chef is tasting each creation to better adjust it to its perfection. I was faced with a dilemma: how could I continue to extract enhancing flavors and still shave off a few pounds? The answer: by discovering the delicious role that great wines can play in healthy cuisine.

Most people don't realize that oils and fats have no flavor in themselves. They do, however, act as an effective vehicle for absorbing and transmitting flavors. By substituting wines for oil, the complex flavors within the wines contribute directly to the dish. For example, white wines can infuse tropical fruit, berry, melon and lemon grass flavors, while red wines can evoke more earthy tones of these flavors plus such spices as clove, cinnamon and anise.

Whenever a recipe calls for oils or fats, experiment with something new. For instance, try a "steam-sauté" technique. Sauté the foods with a very light coating of oil and then finish them by dashing some wine into the pan for a quick steam infusion of flavors.

Raise a glass of Kendall-Jackson wine and toast the pleasures of healthy cuisine. With food – and with wine – It's All About Flavor.

Kendall Jackson Wine Country Store
337 Healdsburg Avenue
Healdsburg, CA 95448
707-433-7102

Chateau St. Jean

one of California's most acclaimed wineries, is also known for its beautiful buildings, manicured gardens and lovely picnic grounds. Inside the historic Chateau, built in 1920, sample award-winning white, red, and late harvest varietal wines, then take a self-guided tour of the winery. Open daily, 10 until 4:30, except major holidays.

8555 Sonoma Highway
Kenwood, CA 95452
707-833-4134

Petaluma Mushroom Farm, Inc.

is a leading supplier of fresh mushrooms in the San Francisco Bay Area. All cultivated mushrooms are a good fiber source, low in calories, and cholesterol free. *Agaricus* contains more potassium than specialty mushrooms, and Shiitake are proportionately high in fiber and protein.

782 Thompson Lane
Petaluma, CA 94952

J Wine Company's

mission is to create elegant, world class wines that reflect the rich terroir of Sonoma County's Russian River Valley and that will enhance the special moments in the lives of our customers. *J Sparkling Wine* is inspired by the finest traditions of Champagne as well as endowed with an esteemed California pedigree.

11447 Old Redwood Hwy.
Healdsburg, CA 95448
707-431-5400

Sonoma Mission Inn and Spa

The 170-room Sonoma Mission Inn and Spa in the heart of California's Wine Country is a luxury resort and European-style spa surrounded by 10 acres of eucalyptus-shaded grounds.

This popular destination at Boyes Hot Springs was originally used as a sacred healing ground by Indians drawn to the underground springs' curative powers. In 1927, the present Sonoma Mission Inn rose from the ashes of a prior resort, and was designed to replicate a California mission.

The Grille is the Inn's premier dining room known for its fresh and innovative Wine Country cuisine, with both indoor and poolside terrace dining.

In addition, the Café features hearty country breakfasts and an eclectic America menu. The Café is Sonoma's oldest continuously operating restaurant, a local favorite for half a century.

P.O. Box 1447
Sonoma, CA 95476-1447
707-938-9000

POULTRY

PAN SEARED DUCKLING WITH WARM RED CABBAGE SALAD

Michael Valmassoi, Center City Diner

1 duckling, whole
¼ head red cabbage, julienned
1 carrot, julienned
1 sprig green onion, chopped
1 teaspoon butter
½ basket blackberries

4 ounces duck glacé
1 teaspoon balsamic vinegar
pinch cracked black
   peppercorns
pinch thyme

Roast duckling medium rare at 400 degrees. Cool. Remove breast meat, whole leg with thigh. Reserve. Roast duck bones until golden brown. Make duck stock and reduce to a glacé. To order, score breast meat and sear to desired temperature. Roast leg and thigh in 400 degree oven. In hot sauté pan add olive oil, cabbage, green onion and carrot. Toss quickly and add balsamic vinegar. Warm duck glacé, add butter, thyme, pepper and blackberries. Place cabbage at bottom of sauté. Slice and fan duck breast. Place on top of cabbage. Spoon sauce over breast meat. Place leg and thigh on plate and garnish with roasted potatoes or baby vegetables.

2 servings

PAPRIKA CHICKEN WITH YOGURT

Dairy Council of California

1 tablespoon olive oil
1 onion, finely chopped
1 tablespoon minced fresh
   ginger
2 cloves garlic, minced
2 tablespoons paprika
Salt & cayenne pepper to taste
pinch sugar

½ pound sliced fresh
   mushrooms
2 tomatoes coarsely chopped
½ cup low-fat plain yogurt
1 pound chicken white meat,
   boned, skinned and
   shredded

In a 10 inch skillet heat olive oil and cook onion, ginger and garlic. Add paprika, salt and cayenne pepper, sugar, mushrooms, tomatoes and yogurt and cook for about 5 minutes. Add chicken to skillet; cook until done.

4 servings

BUTTERMILK MARINATED GRILLED CHICKEN

California Milk Advisory Board

2½-3 pounds boneless, skinless chicken breasts

3 bell peppers (red, yellow and green) cut in 1½ inch squares

Skewers*

MARINADE:

2 cups lowfat buttermilk
½ cup white wine vinegar
4 green onions, finely chopped
4 cloves garlic, minced
1 tablespoon minced fresh rosemary

1 tablespoon olive oil (optional)
½ teaspoon crushed red pepper
½ teaspoon salt
½ teaspoon pepper

In a large bowl, combine marinade ingredients. With palm of hand, flatten chicken to thickness of ⅜ inch. cut into long 1½ inch wide strips. Add chicken to marinade; stir to coat. Cover and refrigerate at least ½ hour or up to 24 hours. Thread chicken onto skewers, ribbon style, alternating with peppers. Spoon extra marinade over chicken. Cook over hot coals or under preheated broiler on foil-lined broiler pan, about 4 minutes per side or until center of chicken is no longer pink.

8 servings.

*Note: If using wooden skewers, soak in water 10 minutes before using.

SWEET BASIL AND SPICY CHICKEN

Gary Chu's Gourmet Chinese Cuisine

8 ounces thin-sliced white chicken meat
3 ounces snow peas
3 ounces fresh small button mushrooms, sliced
8 leaves of sweet basil
½ spicy red pepper

1 clove garlic, minced
½ teaspoon ground ginger
½ tablespoon ShaoXing wine or dry sherry
½ teaspoon salt
Freshly ground pepper
2 tablespoons canola oil

Marinate the chicken in wine for 10 minutes. Heat the wok. Add the canola oil and marinated chicken to wok. Sauté until chicken is done. Take chicken out of the wok and set aside. Put the garlic, ginger and red pepper into the wok, and sauté for 10 seconds. Add snow peas and mushrooms and previously cooked chicken, basil and sprinkling of salt and pepper. Sauté everything together for 15 seconds. Add 1 teaspoon sesame oil.

ShaoXing wine can be purchased in any Asian grocery store.

CHICKEN BREAST FUNGHI (POLLO E FUNGHI)

Randy Hoppe, Catelli's The Rex

4-6 boneless, skinless chicken breasts
12 ounces portabello mushrooms, sliced
12 ounces button mushrooms, sliced
1 tablespoon minced fresh garlic

3 ounces Madeira wine
3 ounces chicken stock, fresh
2 ounces diced tomatoes
2 tablespoons fresh basil chiffonade (ribbons)
2 teaspoons butter

Dredge breast in flour, salt and pepper. Sauté in peanut oil until nearly cooked through. Set aside and keep warm. In same pan add more peanut oil and add both types of mushrooms. Sauté until they begin to sweat, add garlic and sauté one minute. Add Madeira wine. Cook until reduced by half. Add chicken stock and tomatoes. Reduce again. Add breast, butter and fresh basil. When breast is done, place on plate and top with mushroom sauce.

4 servings

MEDITERRANEAN CHICKEN

De Loach Vineyards

12 chicken thighs, skinned and boned

1½ cups De Loach Vineyards Zinfandel or Cabernet Sauvignon

8-10 celery stalks, trimmed and cut into 1 inch pieces

8 large shallots, peeled and quartered

1 cup oil-cured olives, pitted

1 cup golden raisins

½ cup capers, drained

3 tablespoons chopped fresh sage

3 tablespoons fresh rosemary, removed from stems and chopped

1½ teaspoons kosher salt

Freshly ground black pepper to taste

2 tablespoons olive oil or as needed to brown chicken

1 cup chicken stock

⅓ cup tomato paste

Combine chicken, wine, celery, olives, shallots, raisins and capers. Sprinkle with half sage and rosemary, 1 teaspoon salt and pepper. Mix well, cover, refrigerate and marinate overnight. Preheat oven to 350 degrees. Remove the chicken from marinade, reserving liquid. Heat olive oil in a large heavy skillet and sauté chicken until golden. Set aside. Deglaze pan with stock, scraping pan to loosen browned bits. Add tomato paste, remaining sage, rosemary, salt and reserved marinade and bring to a boil. - Remove from heat. Arrange chicken in large oven-proof casserole and add marinade mixture. Transfer pan to oven and bake 45 minutes or until chicken is very tender. Serve over a mixture of fresh corn kernels and orzo pasta with De Loach Vineyards Zinfandel or Cabernet Sauvignon.

Serves 6

STUFFED BREAST OF CHICKEN WITH RICOTTA, CHARD AND HERBS

Lisa Hemenway

3 tablespoons olive oil
4 breasts of chicken, skinless
1 cup Ricotta
1 small yellow onion, minced
1 small leek
2 tablespoons chopped fresh
    basil

8 green chard leaves
½ cup Asiago cheese
Salt and pepper to taste
1 pinch nutmeg
1 cup white wine

Place chicken breasts between plastic wrap and pound to ¼ inch thickness. Set aside. Bring 2 quarts salted water to a boil. Blanch chard leaves about 3 minutes. Pull from hot water and run under cold water. Set aside. Sauté onion with leek for 3 minutes in olive oil. Remove from heat. In small bowl place Ricotta, Asiago, basil, salt, pepper and nutmeg. Blend with spatula. Add sautéed onion and leeks. Take 4 chard leaves and finely chop. Add to mix.

To assemble: Lay one full chard leaf over each chicken breast. Place ¼ of Ricotta mixture on top of each leaf. Roll each breast tightly and lay in a baking pan, seam side down. Sprinkle white wine over breasts. Add salt and pepper, and bake at 375 degrees for 20 minutes. Check at the 10 minute point, and baste the top of the breasts. When finished cooking, remove from oven and let rest for 3 minutes. Slice with sharp knife and fan.

Yield: Serves 4

Topolos Restaurant - Russian River Vineyards   Parkinson '96

71

SAUTÉED MUSCOVY MAGRET WITH HERBS

Junny Gonzalez, Proprietor Chef, Sonoma Foie Gras

Magret is the breast of a duck that has produced foie gras. In this recipe the magret is cooked like a roast, medium rare. Finishing the sauce with foie gras gives it a unique and delicious flavor.

1 pair magret
2 shallots, chopped
3 garlic cloves, chopped
3 tablespoons chopped fresh
    herbs (basil, oregano,
    parsley, tarragon, thyme,
    etc.)
1 tablespoon coarse salt

1 teaspoon freshly cracked
    black pepper
2 tablespoons extra virgin
    olive oil
1 cup duck stock
1 teaspoon sweet butter
1 small piece of foie gras

Mix shallots, garlic, herbs, salt and pepper. Lightly score the magret skin. Rub with olive oil, and dredge in the spice mixture. Wrap the magret in a plastic bag and refrigerate 8 hours or overnight.

Preheat oven to 400 degrees. Wipe most of the marinade off the magret. Sear each side one minute in a sauté pan over medium heat, the sauté, fat side down until the fat is golden brown - about five minutes. Turn over. Roast in preheated oven for 10 to 12 minutes - until medium rare. Remove the magret from the oven and allow it to rest at least five minutes so that the juices are not lost when it is sliced.

Make the sauce while the magret is roasting: Drain all the fat from the sauté pan and deglaze with duck stock. Reduce by about 20% until the sauce just begins to thicken. Mix the butter with foie gras until smooth. Strain through a fine sieve. Swirl in foie gras butter to finish the sauce, verify seasoning, and keep warm. Thinly slice magret on the bias. Fan the slices on warm plates. Top with sauce and serve at once.

Serves 4 to 6 as an entrée.

SAUTÉED FOIE GRAS WITH CRACKED BLACK PEPPER AND HONEY VINEGAR SAUCE

Junny Gonzalez, Proprietor Chef, Sonoma Foie Gras

Sautéed fresh foie gras is truly one of the world's finest delicacies, and is not hard to prepare. There are a few important considerations when sautéing foie gras. First and most important: Use grade "A" livers - only the best livers have the perfectly firm, yet meltingly tender texture to serve hot. Second: Cook the foie gras very quickly, at high heat in a heavy pan. Cooking foie gras at this high heat gives it a little crust on the outside, and is the mark of an expert cook. Be sure to provide adequate ventilation for the smoke. My honey vinegar sauce brings out the best in the foie gras.

Sonoma Foie Gras grade "A"
1 cup duck stock
1 teaspoon honey
1 tablespoon sherry wine
   vinegar
1 tablespoon black
   peppercorns, crushed
Salt

Slice foie gras into ⅜ inch thick medallions. Save small pieces for another use, such as raviolis, foie gras butter, salads, etc. Combine stock, honey and vinegar in a sauce pan, and reduce by about one-fourth - until the sauce begins to thicken slightly. Season with salt and keep warm. Heat a heavy sauté pan over high heat. Season slices of foie gras with salt and sprinkle generously with pepper, lightly pressing pepper into the foie gras. Sear foie gras in the hot pan 20 to 30 seconds per side. The foie gras will render its own fat and shrink a little. It should be a rich golden brown on the outside; pink and meltingly tender on the inside. Blot each foie gras slice on a towel. Mirror four pre-warmed plates with sauce; place foie gras on sauce. A nasturtium makes a beautiful garnish for this dish.

Serves 4 as an entrée.

SAUTÉED CHICKEN
IN CHAMPAGNE SAUCE

Chef Sarah Deane, Korbel Champagne Cellars

6 boneless, skinless chicken breasts

3 tablespoons butter

Melt butter in a sauté pan and cook chicken over medium heat for five minutes each side.

SAUCE:

1 teaspoon minced garlic
1 stick (½ cup) butter
⅓ cup flour
1 cup chicken stock

2 cups heavy cream
1 cup champagne
chopped parsley
paprika

Melt butter and garlic in a heavy sauce pan. Stir in flour. Slowly stir in stock, champagne and cream. Reduce liquid over medium heat by half. Season with salt, pepper and chopped parsley and paprika.

Serve with rice or pasta and vegetable.

ANGELO'S CHICKEN CACCIATORE

Angelo Ibleto, Angelo's Wine Country Deli

A healthy great tasting low fat meal

1 pound chicken cut into pieces
1 onion, chopped
1 bell pepper, chopped
3 tablespoons olive oil

2-3 cloves garlic, chopped
1 can Italian style tomatoes
1 jar Angelo's Italian Salsa
1 cup sliced fresh mushrooms

Brown chicken and garlic cloves in olive oil. Add onion, bell pepper, mushrooms and Angelo's Italian Salsa. Simmer until done, approximately 1 hour. Serve over rice with green salad.

8 servings

CHICKEN SCALLOPINE PEDRONCELLI

Phyllis Pedroncelli, Pedroncelli Winery

3 whole skinned and boned chicken breasts
1 large onion, chopped
1 pound Crimini or button mushrooms, quartered
4-5 garlic cloves, sliced
1½ cup chicken broth, low sodium
1 cup Pedroncelli Primavera Mista (may substitute Chardonnay)
⅓ cup flour plus 1 to 2 tablespoons for sauce
Pure or light olive oil

Slice chicken into three inch strips and dredge in flour seasoned with salt and pepper.

Brown the strips in olive oil using an electric skillet. Remove the chicken and add a bit more olive oil. Sauté onion until soft; add mushrooms and garlic. Continued sautéing until mushrooms are soft and have given up their liquid. Add broth, wine and chicken. Cover and cook for another 15 to 20 minutes on low heat. Add small amount of flour to thicken sauce. Simmer a couple of minutes more. Serve over rice or pasta. Enjoy with a glass of our Primavera Mista or Chardonnay.

CHICKEN MARSALA

James D'Ottavio, Cafe Buon Gusto

Wonderful served over fettucini.

4 chicken breasts
Olive oil
Unsalted butter
Flour
Salt and pepper
Italian seasoning
1½ cups sliced mushrooms
1½ cups good quality sweet Marsala
¾ cup chicken stock
¾ cup heavy cream

In a sauté pan add olive oil and unsalted butter. Dust chicken breasts with seasoned flour (flour, salt, pepper and Italian seasonings). Add to pan and sauté to golden brown. Turn over, add sliced mushrooms and sauté with chicken. Add Marsala and chicken stock. Reduce to one-half, add heavy cream and reduce to sauce consistency.

CHICKEN FRANCESE

Graziano's Ristorante

4 boneless chicken breasts (cut lengthwise and floured)
¼ cup flour
¼ cup cooking oil
1 tablespoon chopped dry shallots

10 medium mushrooms, sliced
pinch salt and white pepper
½ cup sherry
¼ cup butter (½ cube)
1 pint heavy cream

Use medium skillet to heat oil, add floured chicken and let cook on high until golden brown. Remove oil and add shallots, mushrooms, salt and pepper and let cook until shallots are golden brown. Then add sherry, let cook for another 30 seconds. Add cream and butter and continue cooking on low heat until sauce thickens.

4 servings

BREAST OF CHICKEN WITH LENTILS AND SWEET PEPPERS

Bruce Osterlye, Aram's Cafe

Serve with a salad and Jajik.

6 chicken breasts, skinned with bone
3 large onions, sliced
3 green bell peppers
3 red bell peppers
1 cup lentils

2 cups chopped whole tomatoes
1 tablespoon black pepper
½ cup tomato purée
Salt to taste
Olive oil as needed

Roast peppers whole, then peel, seed and slice. Cook onions with olive oil in a large pot. Add roasted peppers, lentils, chopped tomato, tomato purée, salt and black pepper. Add water to cover by about 1 inch. Cook covered in 350 degree oven for about one hour. Grill or broil chicken breasts with light salt and garlic oil. Cook until about ¾ done, then transfer to vegetable pot. Mix well, add water if needed. Continue cooking covered until chicken is done.

Serves 6.

ERNIE'S CHICKEN

Jan Rosen, Executive Chef, J.M. Rosen's Waterfront Grill

This recipe was developed by Jan Rosen as a tribute for Frank Sinatra's long time personal assistant's husband. Mr. Sinatra gave the Tomato Sauce Recipe to Jan Rosen to be used in this dish.

1 medium eggplant
Salt
2 eggs beaten
1 cup bread crumbs (Italian seasoned)
4 boneless chicken breasts

Clarified butter
Flour
Mozzarella cheese
Frank Sinatra's Tomato Sauce (recipe follows)

Peel eggplant and slice into 1 inch rounds. Salt and set aside to remove excess moisture. After several hours rinse well, pat dry and dip eggplant into the two beaten eggs. Heavily dust with Italian seasoned bread crumbs. Sauté until golden.

Lightly dust four chicken breasts with flour. Sauté in clarified butter until each side is seared. Place sautéed eggplant round on top of each breast. Top with Frank Sinatra's Tomato Sauce and Mozzarella cheese. Place in oven for 10 minutes at 400 degrees. Serve to oohs and aahs!

4 servings

FRANK SINATRA'S TOMATO SAUCE RECIPE

Jan Rosen, Executive Chef, J.M. Rosen's Waterfront Grill

2 tablespoons olive oil
¼ onion cut crescent shaped
4 cloves garlic

1 #2½ can of Italian peeled tomatoes
Fresh basil and oregano
Salt and pepper

In a pan heat the olive oil. Add onion and garlic. Sauté until brown and remove the garlic. Put the tomatoes in a blender with a small amount of liquid from the can and mix gently for less than a minute. Slowly add the tomatoes to the mixture in the pan, being very careful pouring the liquid on the oil. Add fresh basil and oregano, salt and pepper and simmer for 15 minutes.

J. M. Rosen's Waterfront Grill

marks a triumphant return to Petaluma's restaurant scene for sisters Jan and Michele Rosen. They started originally in the Great Petaluma Mill in 1976 with The Salad Mill, and opened a second restaurant in 1979 in downtown Napa.

In 1983, they were on their way to West Coast fame when they created their renowned
J. M. Rosen's cheesecake while simultaneously opening their first elegant dinner establishment, J. M. Rosen's in historic Railroad Square in Santa Rosa, and J.M. Rosen's Cheesecake Etc. in the Village in Corte Madera.

By 1989, their cheesecake was sought after in prestigious communities such as Beverly Hills and Palm Springs. Customers included Chasen's and The Beverly Hills Hotel – even the White House featured J. M. Rosen's cheese-cake! Now, their cheesecakes are sold throughout California, Nevada, Washington, Oregon and Washington, D.C.

In 1996, a dramatic location overlooking the Petaluma River was the chief attraction luring the Rosens back to Petaluma. "We couldn't pass on this location," Jan Rosen said, and a new restaurant was born.

J. M. Rosen's Waterfront Grill features excellent cuisine, an extensive wine list, and of course, the famous cheesecake. Both indoor and outdoor-on-the-river seating is available year round.

The restaurant is open Tuesdays through Sundays. Lunch is from 11:30 a.m.-2:30 p.m., dinner is 5:30-9:30 p.m. Brunch on Sundays 11-:30 a.m.-2:30 p.m. Reservations are advised.

(707) 773-3200
54 East Washington Street
Petaluma, CA 94952

Arrowood Vineyards & Winery

This picturesque winery, owned by Richard and Alis Arrowood, is located in Sonoma's historic Valley of the Moon. Richard, long acclaimed as one of California's finest winemakers, produces limited quantities of hand-crafted wines, using only Sonoma County grapes. His goal has been, and will continue to be, to produce wines of singular, exceptional quality - without compromise. Winery open daily - 10 a.m. to 4:30 p.m. ...visitors welcome!

14347 Sonoma Highway
Glen Ellen, CA 95442
Tel: 707-938-5170
FAX: 707-938-5195

Shoffeitt Seasonings

Shoffeitt Gourmet Seasonings range from lemon pepper to chunky bleu cheese salad dressing, with 40 flavors in between. We also have mustards, gourmet oils, jams, vinegars, and so much more. Visit our tasting room and gift shop in the heart of Sonoma County Wine Country and see for yourself how fresh ingredients, mixed in exacting proportions, will make people think you've been in the kitchen all day. See our gift packs and picnic baskets. We ship everywhere. Ask for our free catalog.

208 Healdsburg Avenue
Healdsburg, CA 95448
1-800-533-3855
707-433-5555

Sonoma Foie Gras

has achieved success since its inception, consistently producing foie gras and Muscovy duck products of the highest quality. Silky, rich foie gras, a seductive delicacy, is a highlight of elegant dining. Fine restaurants comprised the firm's original clientele, and in 1991 retail mail order service was established. Nationwide demand from chefs led to addition of a USDA facility in 1992. Fresh Sonoma Foie Gras products are available for delivery anywhere in the country.

P.O. Box 2007
Sonoma, CA 95476
707-938-1229
800-427-4559

Catelli's The Rex Restaurant & Bar

Our rural location in Sonoma County is the perfect setting for a relaxing and enjoyable meal.

The Rex offers traditional Italian cuisine as well as seafood, poultry, steaks and innovative daily specials using fresh local ingredients, an award winning wine list with more than 90 wines. USA Today selected The Rex's tortellini with smoked pork as fourth on their 1996 top ten list of delectable dishes.

Facility choices include our lovely dining room, a beautifully landscaped patio suitable for wedding receptions, a full service bar, and banquet facilities.

Lunches Mon.-Fri., 11:30-2:00. Dinner seven nights a week, reservations recommended.

21047 Geyserville Avenue
Geyserville, CA 95441
707-433-6000

SEAFOOD

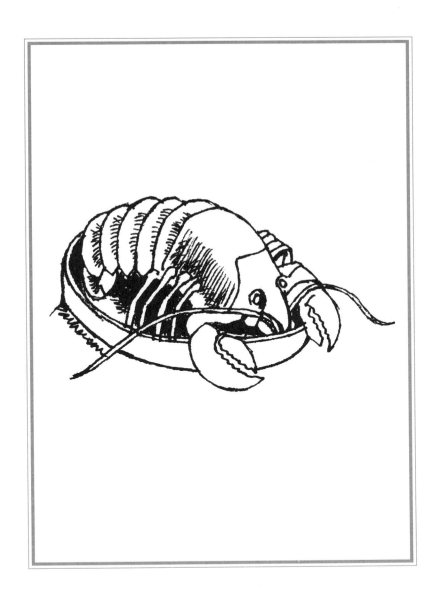

ROASTED MONKFISH WITH CITRUS SAUCE, FRISEE, WATERCRESS AND CRISPY CALAMARI

Chef Toni Sakaguchi, The Grille, Sonoma Mission Inn and Spa

2 pounds monkfish filets, cleaned
1 ounce olive oil
20 ounces Citrus Sauce, recipe follows
2 heads frisee (member of the chicory family)
2 bunches watercress
4 ounces Orange Thai Basil Vinaigrette, recipe follows
1 bunch chives, cut on a bias
1 lime
10 ounces calamari, cleaned and cut in rings
8 ounces Wondra flour
1 lemon, juiced, zest chopped fine
1 cup buttermilk
canola oil for deep frying
salt and pepper to taste

Place the buttermilk and lemon juice in a bowl. Mix. Add the calamari. In a separate container, combine the Wondra and lemon zest. Season with salt and pepper. Set aside.

Heat olive oil in sauté pan. Season monkfish filets with salt and pepper. Place in hot pan. Sear on all sides. Finish in the oven until medium (let rest before slicing).

While the monkfish is cooking, drain the calamari from the buttermilk mixture and dredge in the seasoned Wondra. Shake off excess Wondra. Deep fry until crisp. Drain on paper towels. Season with salt and pepper. Place the frisee, watercress and calamari in a bowl. Add Orange Thai Basil dressing. Toss.

ORANGE AND THAI BASIL VINAIGRETTE:

1½ cup orange juice
½ cup rice wine vinegar
1 tablespoon finely diced shallots
¼ teaspoon finely chopped garlic
½ teaspoon finely chopped ginger
½ bunch Thai basil, finely chopped
1 tablespoon sesame oil
salt and pepper to taste

Combine all ingredients. Season with salt and pepper.

CITRUS SAUCE:
4 ounces sliced shallots
2 cups white wine
1 pound butter

1 each lemon, orange, lime,
  juices (save and chop zest)
salt and pepper to taste
1 teaspoon olive oil

Heat olive oil in pan. Add shallots and sweat, but do not color.
Add white wine and reduce until only ¼ cup remains. Slowly
whisk in the butter to make a butter sauce. Finish with the
citrus juices. Season with salt and pepper. Strain through a fine
chinois. Stir in finely chopped zest.

To Serve: Slice the monkfish on a bias. Pour citrus sauce on the
plate. Turn plate to spread to edges. Place three monkfish slices
a couple of inches from the center of the plate (like the
Mercedes Benz logo). Place salad mixture in the center of the
monkfish. Top with a squeeze of lime. Sprinkle with chives.

Servings: 10.

STEAMED MUSSELS WITH CREAM SAUCE

Carlo Galazzo, The Inn at the Tides Bay View Restaurant

6 pounds fresh mussels
1 medium shallot, finely
  chopped
4 ounces butter
1 cup dry white wine

1 cup heavy cream
½ fresh lemon, juiced
¼ bunch fresh parsley,
  chopped
Salt and white pepper to taste

Scrub mussels thoroughly, make sure they are clean and free of
sand. In a saucepan, bring shallots, butter and white wine to a
simmer. Add mussels to mixture and cover. Turn them gently so
that the mussels are evenly heated. Simmer until all mussels are
open, about 7 to 8 minutes. With a slotted spoon, remove mussels
and place in individual serving bowls or one large serving bowl,
keep warm. Bring wine mixture back to a boil, add the cream,
salt and pepper to taste and lemon juice. Simmer for about 7 to
8 minutes. Strain mixture over mussels and sprinkle parsley.

Serves 6.

PRAWNS TEX-MEX WITH SAFFRON RICE AND RED TOMATO FONDUE

Klaus E. Scheftner, Chef Klaus Catering

Your favorite beer, an assertive white wine or even a light red wine would go well with this dish.

FOR PRAWNS:
24 large or 36 medium raw peeled prawns
1 bunch cilantro, coarsely chopped
1 cup olive oil
1 tablespoon cracked black pepper
2 tablespoons balsamic vinegar
2 tablespoons chopped garlic
6 bamboo skewers (8 to 10"), soak in water

FOR TOMATO FONDUE:
12 ripe fragrant Roma tomatoes, peeled and diced small
1 medium yellow onion, diced very fine
4 ounces butter or olive oil
1 small Jalapeño pepper seeded and diced fine
Salt

FOR RICE:
1 cup long grain rice
1 cup chicken stock
1 cup dry white wine
2 bay leaves
1 small yellow onion diced fine
2 ounces (approximately) butter or olive oil
salt to taste
1 - 2 pinches of saffron

Prawns: *4 hours ahead of serving time*, in a non-reactive bowl, mix cilantro, olive oil, black pepper, vinegar and garlic, then add prawns (patted dry) and coat well. Cover and allow to marinate. *1 hour prior to serving time*, skewer prawns and keep covered. Start your tomato fondue and rice. Pre-heat your barbecue or grill, heat your serving plates. Just before serving time, grill prawns (approximately one minute on each side, depends on how hot the barbecue is), but be careful not to overcook. Brush with leftover marinade while cooking. You may serve this family style or on individual plates. In either case, mound on oval of rice in center of plate surround with fondue and top with skewered prawns, which have been brushed with a very small amount of clarified butter.

Tomato fondue: Sauté onions and peppers in butter or olive oil in a non-reactive pot until opaque. Add tomatoes with liquid and simmer very slowly for 30 to 40 minutes. The result should be a sweet, very thick almost purée-like sauce. Add salt as needed.

Rice: Sauté onions in butter or olive oil until translucent. Do not brown. Add cleaned rice and saffron, glaze over medium heat. Add liquids, bay leaves and salt to taste. Bring to a rolling boil while stirring, immediately cover with a tight fitting lid. Finish in 300 degree oven for 18 to 22 minutes. When done, remove bay leaf and fluff with fork. Keep warm.

Serves 6.

DIJON CRUSTED SALMON FILET WITH CHAMPAGNE-CHIVE SAUCE

Corey Basso, Le Bistro

Salmon filet, 6 ounces to
   8 ounces
Dijon mustard

Corn bread crumbs
Flour
Clarified butter

Lightly coat one side of salmon with Dijon mustard. Press corn bread crumbs on Dijon coated side. Dust with flour. Sear salmon, Dijon side down in a hot pan with clarified butter. Turn and bake at 375 degrees for 2 to 3 minutes.

CHAMPAGNE-CHIVE SAUCE:

1 cup Champagne
¼ cup chopped shallots
2 tablespoons champagne
   vinegar

½ cup heavy cream
½ pound butter cut in small
   cubes
¼ cup chives

In a saucepan put Champagne, shallots and vinegar and reduce until almost dry. Add cream to sauce and reduce by half. Slowly add butter while whisking. Add chives. Keep sauce in warm water bath until salmon is ready.

GRILLED SALMON WITH LAVENDER BUTTER SAUCE

Chef Bea Beasley for Matanzas Creek Winery

6 salmon fillets, about 6 ounces each

1 cup unsalted butter, cut into small pieces

⅓ cup minced shallots

½ cup Matanzas Creek Chardonnay

¼ cup Champagne vinegar

¼ cup fish stock or 2 tablespoons each clam juice and water

1½ tablespoons dried lavender flowers, chopped

¼ cup heavy cream, warmed

Lavender oil (see recipe below)

Lavender grill sticks (optional)

Salt and white pepper to taste

Prepare a fire in the grill. Hydrate lavender grill sticks in water. Rub salmon fillets with a little lavender oil and season with salt and white pepper. Set aside.

In a saucepan, melt 1 tablespoon of butter over low heat and add shallots. Cook until shallots are soft, add Chardonnay, vinegar, stock and lavender flowers. Raise heat to high and cook until liquid is reduced to about four tablespoons. Reduce heat to very low and whisk in remaining butter slowly until it is all incorporated. Stir in warm cream. Strain sauce through fine sieve and season to taste with salt and pepper. Keep sauce warm over simmering water.

Place lavender grill sticks on top of ready coals in grill. When grill grate is very hot, place salmon filets on it. Cook, basting occasionally with lavender oil, approximately 3 to 4 minutes per side or until the fish is firm but not dry. Serve salmon with lavender butter. Garnish with fresh or dried lavender stems with flowers.

Serves 6.

For oven-seared salmon: Preheat oven to 450 degrees. Place a sheet pan in a hot oven for about 5 minutes or until pan is very hot. Brush salmon with lavender oil and place on hot sheet pan. Bake at high heat until salmon is firm but not dry, about 6 to 8 minutes.

LAVENDER OIL:

1 cup grapeseed oil

1½ teaspoon dried lavender flowers

In a small saucepan, heat oil and lavender flowers over low heat for about 8 minutes. Remove from heat, cool and strain.

VIANSA GRILLED PRAWNS WITH CREAMY GARLIC BUTTER

Vicki Sebastiani, Viansa Winery

2 pounds large prawns (16 to 20 per pound)

SAUCE:

½ cup dry white wine, such as Viansa Riserva Anatra Bianco

1 tablespoon plus 2 teaspoons garlic salt

4 tablespoons minced Italian parsley

½ cup freshly squeezed lemon juice

¼ cup freshly grated parmesan cheese

½ cup butter, melted

Remove legs from the prawns. Using a small, sharp knife, slice through the body of the prawn to the shell (without cutting through it). Turn the prawn over onto a flat surface and press the shell side down with the heel of your hand to flatten out the prawn. Rinse the prawns and transfer to a broiler rack, shell side down. Combine the sauce ingredients in a small bowl and whisk vigorously until the wine and butter are emulsified (a thick mayonnaise-like consistency). Spread about 2 teaspoons on each prawn. Use remaining sauce for basting the prawns as they cook, saving some to pass at the table. Reheat and re-emulsify if necessary.

To grill: Place over coals that are not too hot and grill slowly until prawns are pink and have lost their translucence.

To broil: Place 6 to 8 inches below the heat and broil slowly until prawns are pink and have lost their translucence.

Serves 6 to 8

ROASTED HALIBUT WITH MUSHROOMS AND A BASIL SCENTED BROTH

Phillip Breitweiser, Chef, "The Cafe" Sonoma Mission Inn

1 halibut filet
4 ounces Shiitake mushrooms, coarsely chopped
4 ounces Chanterelle mushrooms, coarsely chopped
4 ounces Oyster mushrooms, coarsely chopped
4 ounces Porcini mushrooms, coarsely chopped

2 tablespoons finely chopped shallots
2 ounces finely chopped fresh basil
1 stick lemon zest
1 ounce olive oil
3 ounces butter
Basil broth, recipe to follow

Portion halibut into 5 ounce pieces. Place the olive oil in a large sauté pan over medium heat. Add the halibut and sear until golden brown on that side. Flip the fish over and place into a 400 degree oven and roast another 5 to 7 minutes. Meanwhile melt the butter in another large sauté pan and add the shallots and mushrooms and cook, stirring occasionally, until cooked through, approximately 5 minutes. Season with salt and pepper. Fold the basil into the mushroom mixture. Split the mushroom mixture between 4 plates and place the cooked halibut on top of each group of mushrooms. Surround with the hot Basil broth. Garnish with a sprig of fresh basil.

BASIL BROTH:
2 ounces chopped carrot
2 ounces chopped celery
4 ounces chopped yellow onion
1 bunch fresh basil

2 ounces white wine
2 cups fish stock (see note)
1 ounce butter
Salt and pepper to taste

Melt butter in a medium sized sauce pan. Add the celery, carrot and onion and cook until the onion becomes translucent. Add the white wine and reduce by half. Add the fish stock and reduce by half. Adjust the seasoning. Remove the broth from the heat and put the whole bunch of basil into the pot and cover. Let steep off the heat for at least 30 minutes. Strain through a fine strainer.

If you don't have fish stock substitute clam juice.

4 servings

De Schmie Restaurant - Petaluma

Parkinson '95

TEA AND SPICE SMOKED SHRIMP WITH FUMÉ BLANC MUSTARD SAUCE

Mary Lannin, Murphy-Goode Estate Winery

2 pounds large shrimp, peeled,
cleaned and deveined

MARINADE:
2 tablespoons Fumé Blanc
4 tablespoons soy sauce
1 tablespoon sugar
2 green onions, cut into 2 inch
lengths and bruised with cleaver
4 quarter-sized slices of fresh
ginger, bruised

SMOKING INGREDIENTS:
⅓ cup raw rice
⅓ cup brown sugar
⅓ cup loose orange pekoe tea
2 cinnamon sticks, broken
into small pieces
1 tablespoon dried orange peel
torn into small bits
Turkey roaster with wire rack
Heavy duty aluminum foil

Marinate shrimp in marinade ingredients for about ½ hour. Meanwhile mix smoking ingredients and scatter on several thicknesses of aluminum foil. Arrange shrimp on rack above smoking ingredients. Put lid on roasting pan and position over two burners on top of stove. Turn heat to high and smoke shrimp about 9 minutes or until firm to touch. Open roasting pan outside. Remove shrimp to plastic bag, splash with a dash of Fumé Blanc, and chill. Serve with Fumé Blanc Mustard Sauce.

FUMÉ BLANC MUSTARD SAUCE:
8 ounces Dijon mustard
3 tablespoons sesame oil
2 tablespoons Fumé Blanc
2 tablespoons rice wine
vinegar
⅓ cup coriander leaves

Place all ingredients in food processor and blend.

FRUITI DI MARE

Randy Hoppe, Catelli's The Rex

20 fresh mussels/clams in shell
12 tiger prawns peeled and
  deveined
12 ounces fresh bay scallops
4 ounces clam juice
2 ounces cocktail sauce
1 teaspoon Worcestershire
  sauce
1 teaspoon paprika

½ teaspoon celery seed
½ teaspoon lemon juice
¼ teaspoon Tabasco
½ teaspoon ground
  horseradish
3 ounces heavy cream
16 ounces cooked fettuccine
salt and pepper to taste

Place all ingredients in saucepan. Bring to a boil. Add heavy cream when boiling. When clams/mussels open, whisk in 1 teaspoon butter. Toss juices with 16 ounces cooked fettuccine pasta (cook pasta while seafood is cooking) and arrange seafood on top. Garnish with chopped green scallions.

Serves 4

SALMON GRIGLIATA
CON CILANTRO E CREMA

Chef Michael Ghilarducci, The Depot Hotel Restaurant and Italian Garden

SALMON FILLETS GRILLED WITH CILANTRO AND CREAM

4 6 to 8 ounce salmon fillets
2 tablespoons extra virgin
  olive oil
Salt and pepper
¼ cup chopped shallots
1 tablespoon sweet butter

2 cups dry white wine
1 cup chopped cilantro leaves
2 cups heavy cream
Salt and pepper to taste
Cilantro sprigs for garnish

Marinate the salmon for at least ½ hour in the oil, salt and pepper. Sauté the shallots in the butter. After 2 to 3 minutes add the white wine and reduce until almost all the liquid has evaporated. Add the cream. Bring to a boil and reduce to desired thickness, adjust the seasoning and keep the sauce warm. Broil the salmon scallops to desired doneness. Pour some of the sauce into each of four serving plates. Top with a piece of salmon, garnish with cilantro sprigs and serve.

4 servings.

TROPICAL TANTRUM

Robert Steiner, De Schmire Restaurant, Petaluma

SEARED AHI STEAK WITH PACIFIC THAI SALSA

4 6-ounce #1 Sushi quality
 Ahi steaks, 1 inch thick

8 baby carrots, parboiled 4
 minutes
16 snow peas, parboiled 2 minutes

GARNISH:
1 Belgian endive
1 lemon

1 lime
1 red and 1 yellow beet
 (optional)

SALSA:
Place in blender:
 Several sprigs of fresh basil
  and pineapple sage
 Several leaves of fresh mint
½ bunch of cilantro
4 slices of fresh ginger
2 cloves of garlic
2 jalapeño peppers - seeds
 removed

2 tablespoons capers and juice
1 piece of lemon grass
1 lemon, juice only
1 teaspoon sesame oil
1 teaspoon olive oil
¼ cup tropical fruit juice
 Salt and pepper to taste

Blend on and off for several spins. To this add one chopped
tomato and one chopped roasted red pepper. Sear Ahi for one
minute on each side. When done place in center of plate. Fill
individual Belgian endive leaves with Thai Salsa and arrange on
each side of Ahi steak. Arrange peas and carrots. Add lime and
lemon slice. Put beets through Japanese turning slicer and
decorate plate.

Serves 4

ANGEL HAIR PASTA WITH PRAWNS

Chef Sarah Deane, Korbel Champagne Cellars

Prawns
1 tablespoon chopped garlic
¼ cup chopped parsley
¼ sliced sun dried tomatoes
¼ olive oil

½ cup Korbel Natural
   Champagne
Pasta
Salt and pepper to taste
Asiago cheese

Clean and peel prawns and set aside. Boil two quarts of salted water. While water is coming to a boil, have ready garlic, parsley and sun dried tomatoes. Heat olive oil in a large saute pan. Add the garlic, parsley and tomatoes. Simmer with Korbel Natural Champagne. Turn off heat. Cook pasta as directed on the package (about 3 minutes). While pasta is cooking return heat to saute pan, toss in prawns and cook 1 to 2 minutes. Season with salt and pepper. Drain pasta, toss with prawn mixture and serve immediately. Garnish with grated Asiago cheese.

Jerico . . .
The Hidden Secret of the Best of Sonoma County

From the terraced hillside vineyards to the verdant dairy land that hugs the Sonoma coast, Jerico Products, Inc. plays an integral role in bringing the best of Sonoma County to your table.

You may not know it, but the best wine, dairy products, produce, chicken and eggs produced in Sonoma County have been touched by Jerico. When you sip a gold medal winning chardonnay, Jerico's Pacific Pearl Oyster Shell Flour was used to lime the vineyards, providing the essential calcium for optimum growth and plant health. Your favorite fresh, locally grown fruits and vegetables flourish in soil amended with Pacific Pearl Oyster Shell Flour. Wholesome, versatile Clover dairy products are produced by cows who benefit from the calcium boost provided by Pacific Pearl products, and even your Sunday-best frittata or Eggs Benedict recipe is enhanced by local eggs — which had a greater chance of making it to market with healthier chickens and stronger eggshells as a result of adding Pacific Pearl Lay Blend to the hen's feed.

You may not know Jerico Products, Inc. by name, but when you add up all the local restaurants, bakeries, caterers and home chefs cooking with Sonoma County products, it's clear that Jerico contributes to the quality of life that makes Sonoma County a true gourmet paradise.

100 East "D" St.
Petaluma, CA 94952
707-762-7251 - 707-762-2129

sits elegantly in Bennett Valley, just outside Santa Rosa. Since the first release, the wines from Matanzas Creek have attracted connoisseurs, collectors and wine lovers across the globe. Matanzas Creek Merlot, Chardonnay and Sauvignon Blanc are today among the most coveted wines produced in America. Visitors to the Winery are welcomed not only by outstanding wines, but also by gardens of stunning dimensions. More than 4,500 lavender plants are surrounded by carefully planned gardens filled with rare and beautiful specimens.

6097 Bennett Valley Road
Santa Rosa, CA 95404
707-528-6464

La Crema Winery

Founded in Petaluma in 1978, La Crema is now situated in the heart of the Russian River Valley five miles northwest of Santa Rosa. With its close proximity to the Pacific Ocean and consequent colder growing conditions, the quality of fruit from this region is outstanding. La Crema has quickly become known as one of the area's elite producers of Pinot Noir and Chardonnay, garnering many awards through the years, including the Sweepstakes Award for its 1994 Sonoma Reserve Pinot Noir at the 1996 Sonoma County Harvest Fair, among other top honors.

Chef Brian Leonard invites you to try his recipes which incorporate the wines of La Crema and reflect the flavors of Sonoma County. To taste the full line of La Crema wines, our affiliate California Coast Wine Center is open seven days a week at 5007 Fulton Road. Northbound on U.S. 101, take the River Road exit just north of Santa Rosa, then right on Fulton. Southbound, take the Fulton exit.

Cline Cellars

specializes in Rhone varietal wines. Cline has some of the oldest and rarest vines in California, including a 100-year old plot of Mourvedre grapes. Matt and Fred Cline moved their winery to Sonoma in 1991 and quickly became leaders of California's "Rhone Rangers." Cline has also established an industry reputation for outstanding moderately priced Zinfandel.

24737 Arnold Drive
Sonoma, CA 95476
707-935-4310

Angelo's Wine Country Deli

Angelo Ibleto arrived in Petaluma 30 years ago from Italy. He soon opened his meat market, smoking sausages and gaining fame for smoked turkey, ham and bacon and homemade beef jerky. Angelo's Wine Country Deli offers his own line of Italian salsa, Italian BBQ sauce, marinara, garlic stuffed olives, pickled garlic and spices.

23400 Arnold Drive
(Highway 121)
Sonoma, CA 95476

Bay Bottom Beds,

home of the heavenly Preston Point Miyagi oysters, is a primary supplier of oysters to top Bay Area restaurants and select markets. The owners have pioneered aquaculture techniques that raise each oyster individually, creating a tastier product with a longer shelf life. Bay Bottom Beds harvests upwards of a half million oysters annually.

Bay Bottom Beds, Inc.
Santa Rosa, CA
707-578-6049

Alexander Valley Vineyards

Cyrus Alexander arrived in Northern California seven years before the Gold Rush and settled in the valley named for him. A century and a half later, his homestead enjoys a renaissance as Alexander Valley Vineyards, a leading Sonoma County wine estate. Harry Wetzel Junior (II) and his wife Maggie began planting premium varietal grapes here in 1963, and their son Hank made the first AVV wines in 1975. Today, after 20 plus years experience, Hank is intuitively familiar with his estate grown fruit.

Hank says that "I want to emphasize the natural features of our grapes. My strategy is gentle handling and processing to capture the varietal character and soft tannins."

Alexander Valley Vineyards wines are available for tasting at the winery from 10 a.m to 5:00 p.m. daily.

8644 Highway 128
Healdsburg, CA 95448
(707) 433-7209

MEATS

PINOT NOIR BRAISED LAMB SHANKS WITH POLENTA

Chef Brian Leonard, La Crema Winery

4 tablespoons flour
½ teaspoon salt
¼ teaspoon cracked black
  pepper
4 lamb shanks, about 1
  pound each
2½ tablespoons olive oil
2 cups La Crema Pinot Noir
1 medium yellow onion,
  peeled and thinly sliced
12 cloves garlic, peeled and
  crushed

1 tablespoon fresh thyme
1 tablespoon chopped fresh
  rosemary
2 cups chicken stock,
  preferably homemade or
  low-sodium canned
2 tablespoons cold unsalted
  butter, cut into small pieces
Salt to taste
Freshly ground black pepper to
  taste.

Preheat oven to 425 degrees. Combine the flour, salt and black pepper in a small bowl and lightly dust the lamb shanks with the mixture, shaking to remove any excess. Heat 2 tablespoons of olive oil in a large, heavy roasting pan and bring to the smoking point over high heat. Add the lamb shanks to the pan and brown over high heat, turning to brown evenly on all sides. Remove the shanks from the pan. Heat the additional ½ table-spoon oil in the pan over medium-high heat. Add the onion and garlic and sauté until soft, about 5 minutes, stirring occasionally. Return the shanks to the pan and add the wine. Bring the mixture to a boil over high heat, then reduce to a simmer and continue cooking until the wine has been reduced by half, about 10 minutes. Add the thyme, rosemary and stock to the pan and stir to incorporate. Cover the roasting pan with a tight fitting lid. Place the pan in the oven and bake until the meat is tender and falls from the bone, about 45 minutes to 1 hour. Remove the pan from the oven. Remove the meat from the pan and tent with aluminum foil to keep warm. Place the roasting pan over high heat and bring the liquid to a boil. Cook the sauce until reduced by half, about 5 minutes. Whisk the cold butter into the sauce a bit at a time until emulsified and the sauce thickens. Season the sauce to taste with salt and pepper. Serve the lamb shanks on top of Polenta, and top with the Pinot Noir Sauce.

Yield: 4 main course servings

POLENTA:

4 cups water
1 teaspoon salt

1 cup polenta or coarse ground
   cornmeal
1 tablespoon butter.

Place the water in a large heavy saucepan and bring to a boil over high heat. Add the salt to the boiling water and reduce the heat to a low boil over medium-high heat. Slowly, 1 tablespoon at a time, add the polenta to the boiling water, stirring constantly until all the polenta is added and completely incorporated, about 15 minutes. Continue cooking the polenta over low heat until it thickens and the water is completely absorbed, stirring from time to time. Add the butter to the polenta, stir and cover to keep warm until ready to serve with the Lamb Shanks.

If the polenta thickens too much prior to serving, stir in a small amount of water until it reaches the desired consistency.

Yield: 4 side dish servings

GRILLED LAMB WITH ROUGE SAUCE

Chef Sarah Deane, Korbel Champagne Cellars

2 pounds lamb tenderloins
2 cups olive oil
1 cup Korbel Rouge
   Champagne
1 tablespoon rosemary
1 teaspoon thyme
2 tablespoons minced garlic

Salt and pepper to taste
1 tablespoon butter
2 tablespoons minced shallots
½ bottle Korbel Rouge
   Champagne
4 tablespoons butter
Goat cheese (optional)

Marinate lamb tenderloins in olive oil, Korbel Rouge Champagne, rosemary, thyme, garlic, salt and pepper. Refrigerate 4 hours (up to overnight). In a sauté pan heat 1 tablespoon butter with minced shallots. Add Korbel Rouge Champagne and reduce by half over high heat. Add 2 cups demi glaze, and continue reducing. Finish sauce with 4 tablespoons soft butter, whisk in. (Optional, add goat cheese if desired). Grill lamb tenderloins to desired temperature, about 8 minutes for medium rare. Slice, sauce and serve.

OSSO BUCO IN GREMOLATA

Luca Citti, Cafe Citti

ROASTED VEAL SHANKS IN A GARLIC,
LEMON AND PARSLEY SAUCE

6 pieces veal shank cut about 1 inch thick

1 cup (4 ounces) all purpose flour

2 tablespoons butter

½ cup dry white wine

Salt and freshly ground pepper

1 anchovy filet, chopped

1 lemon, juice and zest

2 tablespoons chopped parsley

Dredge the veal shanks in flour, shaking off excess. Melt the butter in a wide skillet, arrange the veal shanks in it side by side, and brown them on one side over medium heat. Turn carefully and brown the other side. Pour in the wine and allow to evaporate completely. Add salt and pepper, cover and simmer the meat for about 1½ hours, adding water a little at a time to keep some liquid in the bottom of the pan. Add the anchovy and lemon juice and zest. Sprinkle with parsley and serve.

Yield: 6 servings.

ROASTED DOUBLE-CUT LAMB CHOPS WITH A HERB CRUST

Phillip Breitweiser, Chef, "The Cafe" Sonoma Mission Inn

1 lamb loin chop, trimmed

1 ounce fennel seed

1 ounce coriander seed

1 ounce garlic

½ ounce rosemary

½ ounce Italian parsley

2 ounces olive oil

Salt and pepper to taste

Place fennel and coriander seeds, garlic, rosemary, parsley, salt and pepper into a blender bowl and process into a paste. Place the olive oil into a hot sauté pan and then add the lamb and sear all sides. Rub the paste into the top of the lamb rack to make a ¼ inch thick layer. Then place it into the oven at 400 degrees for approximately 15 to 20 minutes, or 130 degrees internal for medium rare. Let rest under a towel (to keep it warm) for about 5 minutes. Then cut it into double chops.

2 servings

GRILLED LEG OF LAMB MARINATED IN VANILLA AND ROSEMARY

Ralph Tingle, Bistro Ralph

A mint au jus goes nicely with this recipe, but is not necessary. Roasted creamer potatoes and roasted garlic cloves mixed with herbs makes a nice rustic complimentary starch.

1 leg of spring lamb, butterflied
½ cup whole fresh rosemary leaves
3 tablespoons chopped mint leaves

6 cloves garlic, finely chopped
6 tablespoons vanilla extract
1 pint vanilla yogurt (with active cultures)

Mix all marinade ingredients in a bowl and evenly coat leg of lamb on both sides. Place in a baking dish to marinate 24-48 hours refrigerated. The active culture yogurt will help to tenderize the meat. Before grilling remove most of the marinade and let lamb rest out of refrigerator to raise to room temperature. Grill over moderately hot coals until medium rare, about 12 minutes per side. Let rest about 10 minutes before slicing thinly and serving.

Serves 8-10

GRILLED NEW YORK STEAK WITH A WILD MUSHROOM BRANDY CREAM SAUCE

Christian Bertrand, Glen Ellen Inn Restaurant

2 8-ounce cuts of lean New York Steak
2 ounces of assorted mushrooms; Shiitake, Blue Oysters, Morels and Golden Chantarelles

¼ cup brandy
1 cup of game stock
½ cup heavy cream

Sauté mushrooms until translucent and deglaze with brandy, stock and cream. Reduce by half. Season the New York steaks with salt and pepper and grill to your preferred temperature.

2 servings

SWEETBREADS THREE WAYS

Robert Steiner, DeSchmire Restaurant, Petaluma

1 pound calves sweetbreads only	1 sliced lemon and juice
Salt	1 onion, quartered
2 bay leaves	3 carrots

Simmer sweetbreads in water with salt, bay leaves, lemon, onion and carrots until tender, approximately 45 minutes. Drain. Place sweetbreads in a flat pan and cool. Reserve stock.

#1 BREADED AND PAN-FRIED
WITH MERLOT REDUCTION:
In small bowl make a mixture of eggs and flour and dip sweetbreads in this batter. Fry in olive oil till golden brown and crisp. Sauté 3 shallots in a tablespoon of butter, add 1 cup merlot wine and simmer till reduced to 1/10. Add demi-glace, soft butter and simmer for 15 minutes. Spoon sauce on a plate, place crisp sweetbreads on top and serve with potatoes and vegetables for dinner.

#2 SWEETBREADS IN CREAM SAUCE:
Take 1 cup of the stock the sweetbreads were cooked in and add ½ cup of cream and ½ stick of butter and reduce to 20%. Add juice of one lemon and 2 tablespoons of capers and juice. Thicken with beurre maniere until nice and creamy and the sauce coats the sweetbreads. For a richer sauce add Hollandaise Sauce. Serve as appetizer or entrée.

#3 SWEETBREAD APPETIZER IN RASPBERRY SAUCE:
Season sweetbreads with salt and pepper and place in puff pastry. Bake in oven until puff pastry is crisp and golden – following package directions. Make a raspberry sauce with 1 cup fresh raspberries (or frozen), add just enough sugar so the raspberries are still on the tart side. Add a little brandy and reduce. Spoon sauce on plate, set sweetbreads on top and garnish with fresh herbs.

ROAST PORK MEDALLIONS WITH CHAMPAGNE CITRUS SAUCE AND BRANDIED MUSHROOMS

Chef Sarah Deane, Korbel Champagne Cellars

1 pork tenderloin, whole	1 tablespoon chopped chives
½ cup orange juice	1 cup sliced mushrooms
¼ cup Korbel Natural	2 minced shallots
1 tablespoon Dijon mustard	½ teaspoon thyme
3 tablespoons white vinegar	¼ cup Korbel Brandy
½ pound butter, cut into pieces	2 tablespoons safflower oil

Heat oil in a sauté pan with shallots. Sear pork on all sides and transfer to a roasting pan. Place in a 350 degree oven for 25 minutes. Add mushrooms to sauté pan and cook gently with brandy, Dijon and thyme. Set aside. In a sauce pan combine juice, vinegar and champagne. Simmer until reduced to a couple of tablespoons. Stir in butter one piece at a time. Keep stirring until all the butter is incorporated. Slice pork medallions and ladle sauce. Top with mushrooms and garnish with chives. *Serve with toasted potatoes and green beans.*

BRAISED LAMB SHOULDER

Bruce Osterlye, Aram's Cafe

2 large onions, sliced	4 cups whole tomatoes, chopped
2 cloves garlic, minced	½ cup white wine
1 large bunch Swiss chard, chopped	½ tablespoon black pepper
3 pounds lamb shoulder pieces	Salt to taste

Cook onions in small amount of olive oil. Add lamb and Swiss chard to onions. Mix. Add tomato, garlic, black pepper and salt to taste. Add water if necessary. Cook covered at 350 degrees for 1½ hours. Lamb should be very tender. Uncover, add wine. Cook 15 minutes longer. Lamb shoulder must be tender and have enough juice for a "sauce" consistency. Serve with rice pilaf, a salad and plain yogurt on the side or Jajik.

6 servings

RANCHO CONTENTO CARNITAS

Patti Baker, Food Columnist Argus Courier, Petaluma

This recipe is a crowd pleaser. You can serve them alone or with stuffed chilies as I do. The fruit salsa and Mango Sour Cream are refreshing and complement the spicy carnitas.

1 8-pound pork butt roast	2 cloves of garlic, sliced
Salt and pepper	2 oranges with skin, sliced
1 large sprig of Epazote	Low-fat milk
(Mexican herb)	Tortillas or Gorditas
1 yellow onion, cut up	

Put salt and pepper on outside of roast. Brown on all sides in a Dutch oven on top of stove. When browned, remove from heat and drain any grease. Place Epazote, onion, garlic and oranges on top and around the roast in the pot. Pour enough low-fat milk to cover three-quarters of the roast. Place a lid on Dutch oven and place in 300 degree oven for about 2 hours. Check to make sure there is enough liquid during this cooking time. Add more milk if needed.

After pork has cooked for 2 hours, add 3 or 4 7-ounce cans of Herdez Salsa Ranchera or Salsa Casera to the meat. (You can use your favorite salsa—hot, hotter or WOW! You need enough moisture so the meat does not dry out.) Pour salsa over top, cover and cook for one more hour or more. Meat should start to fall apart. If you are going to use the same day allow meat to cool and shred apart, removing any extra fatty meat. If you are using next day, you can refrigerate in Dutch oven when meat has cooled. The next day, remove solidified fat and shred meat. Re-heat when ready to serve. This meat will last for several days in the refrigerator.

To serve: This dish is delicious with soft corn tortillas or gorditas, but you can use flour tortillas. Warm each tortilla on a cast iron skillet over high heat. Wrap in dish towel to keep warm. Serve carnitas on a platter or in large serving bowl. Fill tortillas or gorditas with meat and add Mango-Papaya Salsa and Mango Sour Cream and eat like a taco. These are incredibly good.

MANGO-PAPAYA SALSA:

1 mango, peeled, seeded and chopped
1 papaya, peeled, seeded and chopped
1 avocado, peeled, seeded and chopped
1 red onion, chopped
½ bunch cilantro
2 limes, juice only

Chop the above ingredients and place in bowl with lime juice and salt and pepper to taste.

MANGO SOUR CREAM SAUCE:

1 small tub sour cream
1 mango, peeled and seeded
Dash of Tabasco sauce

Blend all ingredients in blender and refrigerate until ready to use. Use fresh cilantro and fresh squeezed lime for the top of each carnitas.

Serves 6 to 8.

LAVENDER ROASTED LAMB

Chef Eric Leonard, Matanzas Creek Winery

Lamb and lavender make a wonderful match. Their forward, unique flavors marry well, suggesting an exotic quality. This recipe is perfect for a summer barbecue or an elegant dinner party.

1 leg of lamb, de-boned
4 Frenched racks of lamb
¼ cup dried lavender flowers
½ cup garlic cloves, crushed
½ cup fresh thyme
½ cup fresh marjoram
½ cup fresh rosemary
¼ cup virgin olive oil
Salt and pepper to taste

Combine lavender, garlic, thyme, marjoram, rosemary and olive oil. Apply mixture to lamb and allow to marinate overnight. Do not allow lamb to marinate for more than 24 hours! Light grill. While waiting for grill to heat, remove lamb from marinade. Season lamb well with salt and pepper. Grill until lamb reaches desired temperature. When lamb begins to emit small pearls of pink juice it has reached medium done. Serve with Matanzas Creek Sonoma Valley Merlot.

4 servings

RONALD'S OLD FASHIONED BEEF POT ROAST

Ronald Waltenspiel, Timbercrest Farms

3 tablespoons olive oil
1 large onion, chopped
5 cloves garlic, minced or
  pressed
¼ cup chopped parsley
½ cup chopped basil leaves (or
  2 tablespoons dried basil)
2 tablespoons chopped fresh
  thyme (or 2 teaspoons dried
  thyme)
3 pound boneless beef roast
  (beef eye of round is good)

1 cup beef broth, regular
  strength
1 cup red wine
¼ cup wine vinegar
10 Sonoma Dried Tomato
  Halves, coarsely snipped
4 medium new potatoes,
  quartered
6 carrots, cut diagonally in
  2 inch pieces
Salt and freshly ground pepper
  to taste

Heat the olive oil in a Dutch oven or oven proof skillet with lid. Add onion, garlic, parsley, basil and thyme and sauté for 10 minutes. Remove from skillet and set aside. Place beef in skillet and brown on all sides, using more oil if needed. Return onion mixture to pan and add broth and wine. Place covered skillet or Dutch oven in 350 degree oven for 1½ hours. Alternatively, cover and allow to barely simmer on low heat, turning meat every 30 minutes (the oven will produce more even heating). Add vinegar and dried tomatoes, potatoes and carrots. Cover and continue to cook for 1 hour longer. Remove meat, potatoes and carrots from skillet and keep warm. Reduce sauce over high heat until it is nicely thickened and add salt and pepper to taste. (Sauce may be strained and thickened with a roux, if desired.) Cut meat into thin slices and place on a serving dish. Surround with the carrots and potatoes. Spoon a little sauce over top and place the remainder in a gravy boat to pass at the table.

6 to 8 servings

SEARED FILET MIGNON WRAPPED IN PANCETTA AND POACHED WITH BÉARNAISE SAUCE

Christian Bertrand, Glen Ellen Inn Restaurant

2 6-ounce prime Filet Mignon
1 ounce pancetta, sliced thinly
1 cup diced vegetables; carrots, celery, red onions

1 teaspoon of sage, thyme and tarragon, chopped and mixed
1 cup Burgundy
½ cup red wine vinegar

Wrap the filet with pancetta around the perimeter, holding it together with toothpicks. Season lightly with salt and pepper. Sear the meat on all sides in a hot pan. Remove and set briefly aside. Add vegetables, red wine vinegar, herbs and Burgundy in the pan. Place the filet on top of the vegetables and poach on low heat to your preferred temperature. Top with Béarnaise sauce.

BÉARNAISE SAUCE:
3 egg yolks
2 tablespoons water
¼ pound butter, diced
pinch cayenne
pinch salt and pepper
dash lemon juice

2 teaspoons chopped fresh tarragon
2 teaspoons chopped shallots
3 teaspoons white wine vinegar

Combine the egg yolks and water in a double boiler and whisk over hot water until well mixed and slightly thickened. Slowly add the butter. When thickened, add the cayenne and lemon juice. Set aside. Combine shallots, tarragon and vinegar and reduce to a glaze. Infuse sauces, add salt and pepper to taste.

2 servings

OLIVE HARVEST LAMB

Michele Anna Jordan

Although olive trees have grown in Sonoma County for over a century, the olive oil industry here is new. It is showing great promise with some of the state's very finest olive oil coming from our county. Olives are harvested in the late fall, not long after the last grapes have been picked, crushed, and fermented. This lamb dish, redolent with the favors of rosemary, garlic, and olives, pays tribute to the county's new olive oil industry.

1 leg of lamb, boned, 5-6 pounds	2 pounds new potatoes
Kosher salt and black pepper in a mill	½ pound carrots, trimmed and cut into 2 inch pieces
Tapenade (recipe on p. 31) or a commercial tapenade	6-8 red shallots
10 rosemary sprigs, 6-8 inches long	15 garlic cloves, unpeeled
	⅓ cup fruity olive oil

Place the leg of lamb on a work surface, fat side up. Remove the fell (outer papery layer) and as much fat as possible. Season with salt and pepper, turn the leg over and spread the tapenade over the inner surface of the lamb. Roll the lamb around the tapenade, folding in the ends and pressing it tightly together. Secure by tying the leg tightly with cotton twine so that it maintains its shape. Tuck the sprigs of rosemary into the twine around the outside of the lamb. Set aside. Place the vegetables in a roasting pan, season with salt and pepper, and drizzle with half of the olive oil. Set a rack over the vegetables so that it rests on the sides of the pan. Place the leg on the rack and drizzle the remaining olive oil over the lamb. Place in an oven preheated to 450 degrees, reduce the heat to 350 degrees and roast for 15 to 20 minutes per pound for rare lamb (about 125 degrees internal temperature).

Remove the lamb and vegetables from the oven and let rest for 15 minutes. Using a slotted spoon, place the vegetables in a serving bowl. Remove the rosemary sprigs and the twine from the lamb, cut the lamb into ¼ inch slices, and arrange it on a serving platter. Some of the tapenade will probably fall out as you slice the lamb; place it on the center of the platter, season the lamb with a few turns of black pepper, garnish with fresh rosemary sprigs, and serve immediately, with the vegetables alongside.

6 to 8 servings

River House

When visiting the Wine Country, your first destination is the gateway city, Petaluma. Located right on the turning basin in the heart of historic downtown you will find a beautiful Queen Anne Victorian, home of River House.

River House celebrates both the creative, culinary excellence of Sonoma County and the architectural history of Petaluma. This circa-1888 registered heritage home was the residence of William Farrell, Mayor of Petaluma in the early 1900s.

River House exudes warmth and hospitality. Relax on the porch with a mint julep and watch the boats go by, or stay for lunch or dinner and enjoy the finest in Sonoma-grown foods and wines. Our American menu is always changing to reflect what is fresh and seasonal. You will love our chef's signature dish, Open Faced Ravioli (as featured in this cookbook) or more traditional fare such as our Sonoma free range Herb Fried Chicken. Whether you are looking for a cozy dinner for two on the patio or a private party for a hundred, River House is your destination in Petaluma.

222 Weller Street
Petaluma, CA 94952
707-769-0123

Food for Thought Market and Deli

provides a vast array of nutritionally valuable, superior quality foods. Support of local producers, organically grown ingredients and sustainable agriculture complements the fresh, delicious foods and natural, environment-friendly products. Locally owned and operated, Food for Thought Market and Deli is dedicated to bringing together producer and consumer in a spirit of partnership, community and trust.

Santa Rosa 707-575-7915
Sebastopol 707-829-9801
Petaluma 707-762-9352

Murphy-Goode Winery

In 1985, grape growers Tim Murphy, Dale Goode and wine merchant Dave Ready founded this family-owned estate winery in Sonoma County's prestigious Alexander Valley. The partners view Murphy-Goode Estate Winery as more than a business – it is a lifestyle. They "have a personal commitment to growing the finest quality grapes and translating them into outstanding wines." Tasting room hours: 10:30 a.m. to 4:30 p.m. daily.

4001 Highway 128
Geyserville, CA 95441
707-431-7644

Café Citti

is owned and operated by Luca and Linda Citti from Lucca, Italy, who blend their culinary heritage with years of experience at John Ash & Co. and Travigne restaurants. Café Citti features traditional home cooking from the Tuscany region of Italy. Menu choices include homemade pastas and soups, salads, lasagne, rotisseried chickens and much more. Try Café Citti – you'll like it. All the local Italians do!

9049 Sonoma Highway 12
Kenwood, CA
707-833-2690

Willie Bird Turkeys

Freshness is not the only thing that makes Willie Bird turkeys so special, For 30 years, the Benedetti brothers Willie and Riley and cousin Rocky Koch have raised Willie Bird turkeys naturally in Sonoma County. The turkeys roam free and eat a healthy diet of natural grains. They receive no growth hormones or unnecessary biotics.

The Benedetti family, the last independent turkey producers in the San Francisco Bay Area, is involved in breeding, broodering, growing and processing turkeys. Their specialty is fresh-from-the-farm turkey. They also operate a Willie Bird Turkey retail store featuring fresh, frozen and smoked turkeys, as well as all other varieties of poultry, the Willie Bird Turkey Restaurant and a UDA processing plant making smoked products, sausage and deli items.

Call our number listed below to learn how you can become part of the Willie Bird Turkey legend!

3350 Sebastopol Road
Santa Rosa, CA 95407
Ph: (707) 545-2812
FAX (707) 575-9036

PASTA

CALIFORNIA-STYLE MACARONI AND CHEESE

California Milk Advisory Board

A slightly more sophisticated variation of traditional macaroni and cheese, this recipe is equally good for a special dinner or family meal. It needs only a green salad or platter of vegetables to accompany it. It is meatless, though diced, cooked chicken, pork or turkey can be added during assembly if desired.

1 pound shell-shaped pasta or dried penne (tubular pasta)
3 cups cold nonfat milk
1½ tablespoons cornstarch
2 cups (8 ounces) grated California Sharp White Cheddar cheese
1½ cups (6 ounces) grated California Monterey Jack cheese
 nonstick cooking spray
2 tablespoons butter
½ pound mushroom caps, quartered

½ cup chopped green onion
1 clove garlic, minced
3 tablespoons flour
1 teaspoon salt
¼ teaspoon ground pepper
½ cup dry sherry
1 cup frozen peas, thawed
1 teaspoon Tabasco green Jalapeño sauce or drops of other pepper sauce to taste
½ cup fresh or dry bread crumbs

Preheat oven to 375 degrees. Coat a 3½ quart baking dish with nonstick cooking spray. Fill large pot three-quarters full of water and bring to boil over high heat. Add pasta shells or penne and cook until tender. Drain in colander, rinse with cold water, then drain again and set aside. In a small bowl, combine milk and cornstarch and whisk until blended and smooth; set aside. In a large bowl, toss grated cheeses together, set aside.

Coat large saucepan with nonstick cooking spray and place over moderate heat. Add butter and, when melted, add mushrooms, onion and garlic; stir frequently for 5 to 7 minutes, or until soft. Add flour and stir constantly for 1 minute; the mixture will be dry. Whisk the milk mixture again, then add to saucepan and whisk until blended. Add salt and pepper and bring to boil, stirring or whisking frequently. Turn heat to low; add sherry, peas and pepper sauce; simmer about 1 minute. Add all but ½ cup of combined cheeses and stir about 30 seconds, or until cheese melts. Remove from heat.

If pasta has stuck together, toss with hands to separate the pieces. Spread in prepared baking dish; pour sauce over pasta and mix to combine and coat evenly. Sprinkle with remaining ½ cup of cheese, then bread crumbs. Bake 30 to 35 minutes, or until golden brown on top and sauce is bubbling.

VARIATION: THREE-CHEESE MACARONI AND CHEESE

Simply by substituting cheeses, this dish becomes a bit richer and creamier capturing the fresh milk flavor of California cheeses. Use 1¼ cups (5 ounces) grated California Cheddar cheese, 1¼ cups (5 ounces) grated Monterey Jack and 1½ cups (6 ounces) grated Mozzarella (part-skim). Assemble and bake as directed above.

FETTUCINI AL FRUTTI DI MARE (FETTUCCINE WITH FRUITS OF THE SEA)

Sandy Poze, Buona Sera Cucina Italiana

1 pound fresh fettuccine
1 tablespoon unsalted butter
1 teaspoon minced shallots
½ teaspoon fresh thyme leaves plus 4 sprigs
¼ teaspoon ground white pepper
½ teaspoon rubbed sage
1 bay leaf
Salt to taste
6 ounces cubed lobster meat (¾ inch cube)

8 ounces cubed salmon filet (¾ inch cube)
2 ounces Sauvignon blanc
4 ounces lobster stock or clam juice
1 Roma tomato, diced
6 ounces Dungeness crabmeat
8 ounces heavy cream
4 ounces cubed Teleme cheese (¾ inch cube)
¼ cup chopped roasted walnuts

In a large sauté pan or skillet, sauté shallots, lobster, salmon, and herbs in butter for one minute. Add wine, stock and tomato. Bring to a boil. Add cream, crabmeat and cheese cubes. Cook until cheese is slightly soft. Serve immediately over cooked pasta in large bowls. Garnish with walnuts and thyme sprigs.

4-6 servings

LEMON-PEPPER FETTUCCINE WITH BAY SCALLOPS AND PRAWNS IN KENDALL JACKSON SAUVIGNON BLANC CREAM SAUCE

Chef Brian Leonard, Kendall-Jackson Winery

While this dish incorporates both butter and cream, they are added in such small amounts (only one tablespoon per serving), that this is not a high calorie item. The citrus flavor from the lemon zest in this recipe really brings out the grassy notes of the Sauvignon Blanc, which I recommend you drink with the finished product.

1 one-pound package lemon-pepper fettuccine	2 tablespoons minced shallots
2 tablespoons softened butter	1 cup Kendall-Jackson Sauvignon Blanc
4 tablespoons flour	4 tablespoons whipping cream
½ teaspoons salt	Salt to taste
1 pound large (16-20 count) shrimp, shelled and deveined	Freshly ground black pepper to taste
½ pound small scallops	2 thinly sliced green onions
1 tablespoon olive oil	Zest of one lemon

Cook the pasta according to the package instructions. Cover and keep warm.

Combine the butter and flour in a small bowl to make a beurre manié and set aside.

Place 3 cups of water in a medium pot over high heat. Add the salt to the water and bring to a low boil. Add the shrimp and scallops to the water and lightly poach until the shrimp begin to turn pink and curl, about 1 to 2 minutes. Remove the seafood with a strainer, cover and keep warm. Reserve the poaching liquid.

Heat the olive oil in a large sauté pain over medium-high heat. Add the shallots and sauté until translucent, about 1 minute, stirring constantly. Add the white wine and cook until reduced by half. Add 1 cup of reserved poaching liquid to the pan and bring to the boil over high heat. Add the reserved beurre manie (butter-flour mixture) to the pan in a tablespoon at a time, until the mixture is smooth and thickened, whisking constantly.

(NOTE: You may not need to use all the butter-flour mixture—use only what is needed to thicken the sauce). Lightly simmer the sauce over medium heat for 3 to 5 minutes. Add the cream and reserved seafood, heating just until warmed through. Season the sauce to taste with salt and pepper, then toss with the cooked lemon-pepper fettuccine. Place the seafood pasta on serving plates and garnish each serving with sliced green onions and lemon zest.

Yield: 6 appetizer servings or 4 main course servings

CONCHIGLIE PETALUMA

SHELL PASTA PETALUMA STYLE
Franco Leicata, Ferruccilo Morassi, Fino Cucina Italiana

1 pound shell pasta	2 garlic cloves, chopped
1 ripe avocado pulp	½ cup cream
2 tablespoons butter	2 tablespoons Parmesan cheese
¼ pound portobello mushrooms	Salt and Pepper to taste

Put the olive oil in the skillet. When hot, add mushrooms, garlic and avocado. Stir well. In a large pot, boil water and add pasta with salt for 7 minutes or until cooked as desired. Drain pasta and mix it together with the other ingredients cooked in the skillet. Stir and add butter, cream and Parmesan cheese. Serve hot.

4 servings

TWISTED PASTA PUTTANESCA

Twisted Vines

3 cups sliced mushrooms
2 tablespoons minced garlic
3 tablespoons minced shallots
2 tablespoons chopped sun-
    dried tomatoes
2 tablespoons chopped capers

¼ cup chopped kalamata
    olives
1 tablespoon minced anchovy
1 tablespoon chopped rosemary
½ cup chopped tomato
½ cup extra virgin olive oil

Sauté above ingredients until mushrooms are cooked. Add
½ bottle white wine   ½ cup chopped red bell pepper
4 cups chicken stock

Simmer for 20 minutes. Before serving over fresh pasta, add
some fresh tomato and basil. Garnish with aged Asiago cheese,
toasted pine nuts and parsley.

4 servings

SPAGHETTI PUTTANESCA

Graziano's Ristorante

1 pound of imported Italian
    spaghetti
3 tablespoons olive oil
2 teaspoons fresh minced
    garlic
6 anchovy filets, chopped
1 teaspoon chopped shallots
1 tablespoon capers

16 Kalamata olives
1 teaspoon crushed hot chili
1 teaspoon white pepper
¼ cup white wine
1 16-ounce can of tomato
    sauce
½ cube butter

In medium skillet heat oil, garlic, anchovies, shallots, capers,
olives and hot chili. Cook for 1 minute on medium heat. Add
white wine, tomato sauce and butter. Simmer for 5 to 10 minutes. Cook pasta and add sauce.

4 servings

Vella Cheese Building – Sonoma

Parham '00

117

OPEN-FACE SMOKED CHICKEN AND WILD MUSHROOM RAVIOLI

Chef Greg Tully, River House

3 12 x 12 inch pasta sheets
12 ounces smoked chicken
 breast
8 ounces wild mushrooms
4 tablespoons olive oil
2 tablespoons chopped garlic
2 tablespoons chopped shallot
1 head fennel, diced
1 large sweet red onion, diced

1 cup diced vine ripened
 tomatoes
¾ cup white wine
12 ounces chicken stock
¼ cup grated Parmesan cheese
4 pieces shaved Parmesan
 cheese
1 bunch organic watercress
Salt and pepper to taste

Cut 12 x 12 pasta sheets into quarters. Cook 3 to 4 minutes or until al dente. Drain and rinse with cold water and coat with olive oil. Slice two 6-ounce smoked chicken breasts on a bias. Heat up large sauté pan with olive oil. Sweat the garlic and shallots. Add the onions, wild mushrooms and tomatoes. When the mushrooms are almost finished cooking, de glaze with white wine. Add the chicken stock and smoked chicken and let reduce by one-half. Add the grated Parmesan and salt and pepper to taste. This completes the filling and sauce.

Place two 4 x 4 inch pieces of the cut pasta sheets on the bottom of the plate. Spoon the hot filling and sauce over the sheets. (This will warm the bottom portion of the ravioli.) Place the third 4 x 4 pasta piece back in the large sauté pan with the hot filling and sauté for final heating. Drape the remaining pasta piece over filling not to cover all filling to give the open face effect. Garnish with sprigs of watercress and shaved Parmesan and enjoy!

PASTICHIO

Engel Recipes, Topolos' Russian River Vineyards and Restaurant

The following recipe is from the forthcoming cookbook *A La Grecque* by Bob Engel and Christine Topolos published by Full Circle Press.

¼ cup butter
2 onions, diced (about 3 cups)
2 tablespoons minced garlic
1½ pounds ground beef or
lamb or a mixture

2 cups diced tomato, fresh or
canned
¼ cup tomato paste
½ teaspoon cinnamon
Greek seasoning or salt and
pepper to taste

Sauté the onion and garlic in the butter over medium heat, then add the ground meat and continue cooking until the meat is lightly browned. Add the tomatoes, tomato paste and seasonings. Cook 10 minutes longer.
1 pound macaroni, ziti, or mostaciolli

Cook the pasta according to package directions. Drain well.
½ cup butter
½ cup flour
4 cups milk
Salt and white pepper to taste

5 whole eggs
1 cup grated Kasseri,
Kefalotyri or Romano
cheese

Melt the butter over medium low heat, stir in the flour and cook for 5 minutes. Whisk in the milk, stirring constantly, bring to the simmer and cook about 10 minutes. The sauce will be fairly thick. Remove the sauce from the heat, add a little sauce to the beaten eggs, then whisk the eggs back into the remaining sauce. Finally stir in one cup of grated cheese.

YOU'LL ALSO NEED:
2 more cups grated Kasseri, Kefalotyri or Romano cheese
A little more cinnamon to sprinkle on top

To assemble the dish: Lightly butter a 9 x 13 inch casserole and put half the pasta in the bottom, sprinkle with one cup of cheese. Next put in all the tomato sauce and again sprinkle with cheese. Top this with the remaining pasta and then the cream sauce. Sprinkle the top very lightly with cinnamon. Bake in a 325 degree oven for 45 minutes or until the top is lightly browned. Allow to cool 10 minutes before serving.
This is sort of a Greek macaroni and cheese with a meat filling. Sound strange? Tastes great!

8 servings (more as a side dish)

FETTUCCINE WITH SMOKED CHICKEN AND ORANGE TARRAGON SAUCE

Willie Bird Turkeys

1 10 ounce package lemon pepper fettuccine
2 tablespoons butter
1½ teaspoons (1 to 2 cloves) minced garlic
½ teaspoon finely minced orange zest
½ cup fresh orange juice
¾ cup chicken stock
3 teaspoons cornstarch dissolved in 3 teaspoons water or stock
10 ounces smoked chicken breast, sliced in 1" julienne
2 tablespoons finely chopped fresh tarragon (or 2 teaspoons dried)
Salt and white pepper to taste

Bring a large pot of water to boil, add pasta and cook 10 to 12 minutes. Drain. Prepare sauce while pasta is cooking. Heat small sauce pan over medium high heat, add and melt 1 tablespoon butter. Add garlic and orange zest. Cook quickly just until garlic starts to brown, 2 to 3 minutes. Immediately add orange juice and stock, bring to boil, boil for 2 minutes. Reduce heat and slowly add cornstarch mixture, whisking to prevent lumps. Add chicken and heat through. Remove from heat and whisk in remaining 1 tablespoon butter (cut into 4 pieces). Season with salt and white pepper. Stir in 1½ tablespoon fresh or 1½ teaspoon dried tarragon. Toss sauce with pasta. Garnish with remaining tarragon.

4 servings

"CALIFORNIA GOLD" PASTA

Vella Cheese Company

1 pound pasta
½ pound butter, melted
1½ cups grated Dry Jack cheese
Salt and pepper to taste

Cook the pasta in boiling water until tender. Drain. Place the pasta in a heated dish. Toss with the melted butter, salt and pepper and grated Dry Jack. Serve with salad and French bread.

COUNTRY PASTA WITH CHARD

Elena Vella, Vella Cheese Company

This colorful combination can stand alone as a main dish or accompany roast chicken, barbecued meat, or fish. "Everyone in my family likes this one," Ig Vella reports.

1 pound Swiss chard
1 cup chopped pecan halves
1 pound bacon
2½ cups dry short-tube pasta
3 cloves garlic, pressed

½ teaspoon crushed dried hot pepper
1 teaspoon Dijon mustard
3 teaspoons wine vinegar
2 cups grated Dry Jack cheese

Wash and drain the greens. Trim off and discard the tips of the chard stems. Slice the stems and leaves fine, keeping them separate. In a large frying pan over medium heat, stir the pecans frequently until they are a slightly darker brown, about five minutes. Pour them out and set them aside. Cook the bacon until it is brown and crisp, then drain and crumble the slices. Boil water in a 5 to 6 quart pan. Add the pasta and cook, uncovered, until tender. While the pasta cooks, discard all but 6 tablespoons of fat from the frying pan. Add the chard stems, garlic and hot pepper to the pan, stirring often until the stems are limp, about ten minutes. Add the leaves and stir until tender. Put the Dijon mustard and wine vinegar in a large bowl and mix in the drained pasta, then the grated Dry Jack, the greens and the bacon. Sprinkle the nuts on top.

Serves 4 to 6.

Jordan Winery

Northern California is a mecca for wine lovers. Many visitors to the area are interested in touring a well-established winery, and of course, sampling wines where they are made can be a truly memorable experience.

Jordan Vineyard & Winery, founded by successful geologist and wine connoisseur Tom Jordan in 1972, is a privately-owned estate organized in the manner of a traditional French Chateau.

From the start, both Jordan Cabernet Sauvignon and Jordan Chardonnay have been made in such a way that they are round, fragrant and approachable upon release, but have the capacity to age beautifully. Jordan wines have gained an international reputation for excellence, a reputation they continue to uphold.

We take pride in showing our facility to visitors by appointment only. Informative tours are given daily at 10:00 a.m. and 1:00 P.M. followed by a special tasting. Wine may be purchased Monday through Saturday, from 8:00 a.m. to 5:00 p.m. Many older vintages and larger bottles are available for purchase exclusively through the winery.

Located in northern Sonoma County, five miles northeast of the town of Healdsburg, Jordan Winery is easily accessible from Highway 101 or Route 128. Please call 707-431-5250 for advance reservations. Experience the difference in Jordan; your welcome is assured.

1474 Alexander Valley Road
Healdsburg, CA 95448
707-431-5250

Twisted Vines

offers something you'll see nowhere else – a wine bar, nationwide personal wine merchant, retail wine shop, and a great restaurant (with no markup on wines) under one roof. With one stop you can taste a wine, send a gift, and have a great meal. Our menu offerings are highly praised. Almost exclusively, we use Sonoma County products – except for fish flown in fresh daily from Hawaii!

16 Kentucky Street
(In the LanMart)
Petaluma, CA 94952
707-766-8162

Lisa Hemenway's Restaurant

is a dinner destination for many local winery personnel hoping to impress their out-of-town guests, as well as a sought-after lunch stop. The cuisine is known for its fresh approaches to international favorites, and her recipes reflect her travels to Bangkok, Singapore, Indonesia, France and New Orleans. Award winning wine list.

714 Village Court
Montgomery Village
Santa Rosa, CA 95405
Restaurant: 526-5111
Tote Cuisine: 578-0898

Vella Cheese Company of California

is celebrating its 65th anniversary of making cheese. Vella is the 1995-96 US Cheese Champion for its Monterey Dry Jack – Special Select, a hard cheese with a rich, nutty flavor. Vella is also known for its High Moisture Montereys along with a wide variety of Cheddars. Group tours are available upon request. Vella is open seven days a week and all products are available through mail order.

315 Second Street East
Sonoma, CA 95476
1-800-846-0505

Kenwood Vineyards
A Family Affair

In 1970, brothers Marty and Mike Lee and brother-in-law John Sheela bought the Pagani Brother's winery, and founded Kenwood. They set a goal of 50,000 cases of wine a year, never dreaming that in a quarter century they would be selling 200,000 cases.

Kenwood is known for its full line of award-winning Cabernet, Zinfandel, Merlot, Pinot Noir, Chardonnay and Sauvignon Blanc wines. Its Artist Series Cabernet Sauvignon has become an annual collector's item. Demand for its Jack London Ranch wines far exceeds supply.

The Kenwood tasting room is open daily from 10:00 a.m. to 4:30 p.m.

Kenwood Vineyards
9592 Sonoma Highway
Kenwood, CA 95452

Bodega Goat Cheese

is a distinctive Peruvian style Goat Cheese, 100% whole pasteurized goat milk, herbs and sea salt with no animal rennet or additives.

Each step in the cheese's production, from pasture to market, insures freshness, full flavor and a unique, natural, handcrafted product. The fastidious adherence to quality production responds to the rigorous demands of California gourmet shoppers who want to know where their food originated, and how it is made. Our present permaculture project is the consumer's assurance of quality as we move toward 100% sustainable, organic agriculture.

This versatile goat cheese is adaptable to any recipe calling for a stuffing cheese, a melting cheese or a cream cheese.

Javier and Patty Salmon
P.O. Box 223
Bodega, CA 94922
876-3483
FAX 707-829-8606

Spectrum Naturals
Great Company In Your Kitchen

Since 1986, Spectrum Naturals has been a leader in providing *consumers the best tasting oils and condiments* on the market.

Spectrum Naturals' healthy oils are all Pure Pressed™ without chemicals and retain all the goodness and flavor with which Nature endowed them.

When you need fine cooking oils, flavorful organic vinegars, intensely flavored seasoning oils, organic, fat free and low fat salad dressings or a heart-healthy canola spread – reach for the leader, Spectrum Naturals.

133 Copeland Street
Petaluma, CA 94952
707-778-8900

MORE SPECIALTIES

POTATO GRATIN

Phillip Breitweiser, Chef, "The Cafe" Sonoma Mission Inn

6 Russet potatoes, peeled
1½ tablespoons butter
1½ teaspoons chopped garlic
¾ cup cream

1 tablespoon chopped shallot
1½ teaspoons chopped thyme
½ cup grated Parmesan cheese
Salt and pepper

Butter a 9 x 9 inch baking dish, sprinkle with the shallots, garlic and thyme. Season to taste with salt and pepper. Thinly slice the potatoes, 1/16 inch thick. Layer potatoes in the pan, alternating the layers with cheese, garlic, herbs, salt and pepper*. Pour cream over the top. Cover with foil and bake for one hour in a pre-heated oven at 400 degrees. After one hour remove the foil, sprinkle on more cheese and brown the top for ten minutes more.

* Only use pepper on every third layer—otherwise it gets too strong.

14 servings.

SWEET POTATO BISCUITS

Spectrum Naturals, Chef Gary Jenanyan

1 cup unbleached white flour
1 cup whole wheat pastry flour
1 tablespoon baking powder
½ teaspoon sea salt
⅓ cup Spectrum Naturals
    canola oil

¾ cup sweet potato, peel
    removed, cooked and
    mashed
2 teaspoons maple syrup
1-2 tablespoons milk
Pinch of cinnamon

Sift dry ingredients together. Place dry sifted ingredients into food processor, add oil and blend. Blend sweet potatoes into mixture. Add a small amount of milk at a time, until dough begins to form into a ball. Process as little as possible. Place dough ball onto lightly floured surface and knead lightly, 5 to 10 times. Roll out into ¾ inch thickness, cut into rounds. Place cut out biscuits on lightly oiled cookie sheet and bake for about 12 minutes at 450 degrees.

12 biscuits

PATATE AL FORNO

Chef Michael Ghilarducci, The Depot Hotel Restaurant and
Italian Garden

Potatoes baked in the oven with cheese and herbs

4 medium potatoes, peeled and
   sliced very thin
2 cups cream
1 egg
 Salt, pepper and nutmeg to
   taste

¼ pound Gruyère cheese,
   grated
1 garlic clove
4 tablespoons soft butter
1 tablespoon mixed fresh herbs
   (rosemary, thyme, oregano),
   finely chopped

In a bowl beat the eggs with the cream and add the seasonings
to taste. Stir in two-thirds of the grated cheese, reserving the
rest. Mix the potatoes gently into the cream mixture. Select a
baking dish that is big enough so that the potato mixture will fill
in no more that 2 inches deep. Rub the baking dish thoroughly
with the garlic clove and then butter the pan well with 1
tablespoon of the butter. Pour the potato-cream mixture into
the prepared pan. Sprinkle the top of the potatoes with the
remaining one-third of the cheese and the herbs and then dot
with the remaining butter. Bake at 325 degrees for one hour, or
until tender. Keep warm until ready to serve. Serves 4 to 6.

JAJIK (YOGURT SIDE DISH)

Bruce Osterlye, Aram's Cafe

1 32 ounce container Low-Fat
   Natural Yogurt
2 cloves of garlic, crushed fine
½ medium cucumber, one-half
   of skin removed in strips
   and diced fine

½ teaspoon dried mint or
   ⅛ cup fresh mint chopped
½ teaspoon salt

Add garlic and salt to a large bowl. Mix well with wire whisk.
Add yogurt, mint, cucumber. Mix with wire whisk. Chill. Add
½ cup crushed ice, transfer to serving bowl, let stand 15
minutes, mix with large spoon, then serve.

*This side dish can accompany any lamb or chicken dish and many
braised vegetable dishes.*

RISOTTO AL LIMONE

Chef Dan Della Santina

6 - 7 cups of chicken broth
(some may be left over)
2 tablespoons extra virgin
olive oil
1 small onion, peeled and
finely diced
1 pound (about 2 cups)
arborio rice (do not wash it)

salt and freshly ground black
pepper to taste
¾ cup grated parmigiano
cheese
½ cup heavy cream, heated
zest of one large Meyer lemon
or regular lemon
juice of ½ lemon
3 tablespoons unsalted butter

Bring the broth to a simmer while you heat the olive oil in a
saucepan over medium heat. Add the onion and sauté until the
onion is translucent (about 3 minutes). Add the rice and stir
well for about 2 minutes so that the rice absorbs the oil. Add salt
and pepper and stir well. Adjust the heat so that the rice is
cooking at a low boil. Add ⅔ cup of simmering broth and stir
continuously. As the broth is absorbed, add more simmering
broth, keeping the rice moist but not wet. Total cooking time
should be 16 to 18 minutes, until the rice is al dente (still firm).
Near the end of the cooking time add the heated heavy cream
in place of the broth. Add the lemon zest and juice and stir well.
Stir in about ½ cup of the cheese and the butter.

Serve immediately on warm plates with the additional cheese to
sprinkle on.

POLENTA

De Loach Vineyards

1½ cups milk
1½ cups chicken broth
1 tablespoon butter
1 teaspoon sugar

½ teaspoon salt
1 cup stone-ground yellow
cornmeal
3 tablespoons unsalted butter

Melt butter in a heavy-weight, deep saucepan. Add milk, sugar,
salt and broth and heat just to boiling. Measure cornmeal and
slowly pour into liquid in a thin stream whisking constantly.
Polenta bubbles and splatters while cooking, so be careful!
Continue to whisk until polenta begins to draw away from the
sides of the pan, about 10-15 minutes. Serve immediately.

Serves 6

SPRINGTIME YOGURT MASHED POTATOES

California Milk Advisory Board

Light mashed potatoes with a mild garlic flavor and softly melted California Cheddar cheese. These can be made ahead, reheated, and browned under a hot broiler just before serving. And don't be startled by the amount of garlic, it becomes delicate and gentle in cooking.

2 pounds new potatoes (about 16 - 20), small red or golden
8 - 10 large cloves garlic, peeled
1½ teaspoon salt
1¼ cup plain yogurt
¼ teaspoon freshly ground pepper
1 cup finely diced California Cheddar cheese (4 ounces)
3 green onions, thinly sliced

Butter 1½ quart baking dish, or other sizable baking dish about 2 inches deep.

Cut potatoes in half, or into quarters if they are large, and place in large saucepan with the garlic. Add cold water to cover the potatoes and garlic by about 2 inches. Add 1 teaspoon salt and bring to boil over high heat. Reduce heat to low, cover the pan partially and simmer until potatoes are tender when pierced, about 20 minutes. Drain off liquid, leaving potatoes and garlic in pan. Add yogurt, pepper and ½ teaspoon of salt. Mash vigorously until potatoes are smooth. Add cheese and green onion and stir just to combine. Spread potatoes in prepared baking dish and brown under the broiler as directed below. If you are preparing potatoes ahead of time, cool to room temperature then cover and refrigerate. Uncover and reheat in a preheated 325 degree oven before browning. Before serving, place potatoes under hot broiler for 3 - 5 minutes, or until lightly browned on top.

6 servings

POLENTA WITH
WILD MUSHROOM RAGOÛT

Mary Evely, Chef, Simi Winery

1½ cups polenta
6 cups water
1 teaspoon salt
4 tablespoons unsalted butter
½ ounce dried porcini
1 small onion, chopped fine
3 shallots, minced
3 tablespoons unsalted butter

4 ounces sliced white
  mushrooms
8 ounces sliced wild
  mushrooms—shiitake,
  oyster, chanterelle
½ cup Chardonnay
⅓ cup Italian parsley, chopped
1 cup heavy cream
Salt and pepper to taste

Stir salt and polenta into water in a 2-quart glass bowl. Place in microwave and cook on high for 10 minutes. Stir well, then cook for another 10 minutes. While polenta is cooking, let dried mushrooms soak in boiling water for 10 minutes. Drain, reserving liquid, and chop the mushrooms. Strain the soaking liquid through cheesecloth and set aside. Sauté the onion and shallots in the butter over medium heat for three minutes. Raise the heat and add the fresh and dried mushrooms and cook until any liquid released has evaporated. Add the Chardonnay and mushroom soaking liquid to the pan and cook down to about ¼ cup. Add parsley and cream and cook until sauce begins to thicken. Season to taste with salt and pepper. Spoon polenta onto warmed plates, top with sauce and serve.

Serves 6.

For a more elegant presentation, make polenta cups by chilling mixture in a buttered 7" x 11" pan. Unmold and cut into six large rounds with a biscuit cutter. With a smaller cutter, make a well in the center of each round, brush with butter and reheat in a 400 degree oven for 10 to 15 minutes. Fill the cups with the mushroom ragoût and garnish with sautéed mushroom slices.

SPICY BLACK BEANS
WITH TOMATO AND CILANTRO

Spectrum Naturals, Chef Gary Jenanyan

2 cups dry black beans
1 red onion, diced
4 garlic cloves, minced
4 tablespoons chopped
    cilantro
1 medium ripe tomato, diced

1 tablespoon lime juice
1 tablespoon Spectrum World
    Cuisine Southwestern Oil
Salt and fresh ground pepper
    to taste

Measure the beans into a 4-quart sauce pan and cover with water. Bring to a boil for 2 minutes. Remove from heat and let stand for one hour or more. Meanwhile, prepare the other ingredients. Drain the beans then cover them with clear cold water. Bring to a simmer, add onions, garlic and oil. Simmer gently for 40 minutes or until tender. Season with salt and pepper. Continue to simmer until beans are thoroughly cooked, adding more water if necessary. Stir in the tomato, cilantro and lime juice. Correct seasoning and serve.

4 servings

RATATOUILLE

Phillip Breitweiser, Chef, "The Cafe" Sonoma Mission Inn

1½ pounds eggplant, peeled
    and diced
1 pound diced zucchini
1 pound diced yellow squash
1 green bell pepper, diced
1 red bell pepper, diced
1½ cups diced yellow onion
2 teaspoons finely chopped
    garlic

¼ cup olive oil
4 large red ripe tomatoes,
    peeled, seeded & chopped
2 ounces chopped fresh basil
1 ounce chopped fresh
    oregano
1 ounce chopped fresh thyme
Salt and pepper to taste

Sauté the eggplant separately. Sauté the two squashes separately. Sauté the bell peppers and the onion separately. Use an equal amount of olive oil and garlic when doing each sauté. Place all the vegetables, herbs and tomatoes together in a large bowl and fold together. Then season to taste.

12 servings

SONOMA CASSOULET

WHITE BEANS WITH LAMB AND DUCK
Michele Anna Jordan

This cassoulet, inspired by the succulent smoked duck produced in our area, is simpler than French versions, in which preserved meats such as goose and duck confit contribute essential flavors. Here, an evocative depth of flavor is provided by a simple stock made from the smoked duck. Although it is not an essential ingredient, the cassoulet is transformed—and takes on a specifically Sonoma character—when it is used. Other than the stock, ingredients may be varied to suit individual preferences and what is available. Omit the smoked or fresh lamb, add 4 duck legs or sausages—especially lamb or duck—or marinate the lamb first in fresh apple juice and sauté a diced apple or two (peeled, of course), adding it with the garlic.

1 pound cannellini beans, Great Northern white beans, or small white beans	¾ pound diced smoked duck meat
¼ cup duck fat (from smoked duck, if available)	1 pound lamb meat, cut in 1 inch cubes, or 4 small lamb chops, fat removed
1 medium yellow onion, diced	1½ cups bread crumbs, fresh
1 garlic bulb, cloves peeled and minced	1½ cups (4-6 ounces) grated dry jack cheese
½ pound smoked lamb, sliced (optional)	1½ quarts simple smoked duck stock*

The night before preparing the cassoulet, place the white beans in a large pot, cover with water, and set aside to soak. If you have not already done so, prepare the duck stock.

To make the cassoulet, melt the duck fat in a heavy skillet and sauté the onions over medium heat until soft and transparent, about 15 minutes. Add the garlic, sauté another 2 minutes, and set aside. Drain and rinse the beans, place them in a large bowl, and toss together the onions and garlic, and any of the sliced or diced meat you are using. If using duck legs or sausages, set them in the bottom of a large oven-proof dish, along with the lamb chops. Top with the bean mixture and spread it evenly in the dish. Pour the duck stock over the mixture. Toss together the bread crumbs and cheese and spread across the surface of the beans. Bake, tightly covered, in a 325 degree oven for 2½ hours, until the beans are plump and tender, removing the lid of the baking dish for the final 20 minutes of cooking. Remove the cassoulet from the oven and let rest 10 minutes before serving.

*To make simple duck stock, simmer 2 smoked duck carcasses and water to cover in a large stock pot for 3 hours. Strain the stock, chill, skim the fat from the surface and reserve it for other uses, simmer the stock again until it is reduced by ⅓, and strain through a fine sieve. let the stock cool, and then store it in the refrigerator for up to 5 days. The stock may also be frozen.

4-6 servings

©1997 Michele Anna Jordan, recipe appears in *California Home Cooking* (Harvard Common Press, 1997)

PATATE PURÉE ALL'ACCIUGHE (ANCHOVIES MASHED POTATOES)

Luca Citti, Cafe Citti

3 large russet potatoes
6 tablespoons unsalted butter
½ medium onion, finely
  chopped
6 flat anchovy filets, rinsed,
  dried and minced

½ cup milk
3 tablespoons heavy cream
Salt and freshly ground pepper
3 tablespoons minced red
  onions

Peel the potatoes and cut them into 1 inch chunks. Steam the potatoes, covered, until very tender, about 20 minutes. Press the potatoes through a ricer or the medium disk of a food mill set over a bowl. In a large nonreactive saucepan, melt 4 tablespoons of the butter. Add the onion and cook over moderately low heat, stirring, until softened. Add the anchovies and stir until melted. Stir in the milk and heavy cream, season with salt and pepper and bring to a simmer. Add the potatoes and stir until smooth and warmed through. Stir in the red onions and the remaining 2 tablespoons butter and serve hot.

Yield: 6 servings

SONOMA RISOTTO WITH LEEKS AND TOME

Michele Anna Jordan

I developed this risotto to highlight tome, a hard, aged chevre, perfect for grating, that is one of my favorite Sonoma county ingredients and also one of the hardest to procure. If you find some, this simple risotto is the perfect showcase for its delicate flavor and texture. If it is unavailable, an aged Asiago will produce excellent, though different, results.

4 medium leeks, white and pale green parts only, thoroughly cleaned and trimmed

4 tablespoons olive oil

2 tablespoons butter

1¼ cup Arborio rice

5 cups homemade duck or chicken stock, hot

4 ounces grated tome or aged Italian Asiago

Kosher salt and freshly ground black pepper

½ pound haricots verts or very young Blue Lake green beans (optional), blanched.

Cut the leeks into thin rounds. Heat 3 tablespoons of the olive oil and butter together in a large skillet until the butter is completely melted. Add the leeks and sauté over medium heat until they are completely wilted, about 10 minutes. Add the rice and stir continuously with a wooden spoon for 3 minutes. Add hot stock ½ cup at a time, stirring after each addition until the liquid is nearly completely absorbed. Continue to add stock and stir until the rice is tender, about 18-20 minutes total cooking time. Have a small skillet ready nearby, with the remaining tablespoon of olive oil. Just before the final addition of stock, set the skillet over medium heat, add the blanched beans, and sauté quickly to heat through. Remove from the heat and keep warm. Stir the tome into the risotto, taste it, season with salt and pepper, and stir in the last of the liquid. Divide the risotto among 4 serving plates or bowls and add some of the beans to each serving. Add a few turns of black pepper and serve immediately.

4 to 6 servings

Depot Hotel — Sonoma

Palummi '88

135

TORTA CON FUNGHI E PANCETTA

Chef Michael Ghilarducci, The Depot Hotel Restaurant and
Italian Garden

Italian-style quiche with porcini mushrooms and cured Italian bacon

CRUST:

4 ounces pancetta bacon, diced very fine

2½ cups flour

2½ cubes very soft sweet butter

¼ teaspoon salt

Sauté pancetta over medium heat until well cooked. Drain and
reserve. In a mixing bowl blend flour with butter and salt—just
until a loose dough is formed and then knead in the pancetta.
Roll out on a floured surface and line the cheesecake or tart pan.

FILLING:

2 ounces dried porcini mushrooms, soaked ½ hour in warm water and chopped

1 tablespoon shallots

1 tablespoon butter

5 eggs

2½ cups heavy cream

½ pound Gruyère or Fontina cheese, grated

Salt, white pepper, and nutmeg to taste

Line the pie crust with buttered foil and fill with beans or pie
weights. Prebake the crust at 375 degrees for 15 minutes. Meanwhile, sauté the mushrooms with the shallots and butter.
Sprinkle the mushroom-shallot mixture over the prebaked crust.
Beat the eggs well, and then beat in the cream, cheese and
season to taste. Pour the cream mixture into the prepared crust
and bake in the top half of the oven at 375 degrees for 25 to 45
minutes, depending on the depth of the pan used. The custard is
done when a skewer inserted into the middle comes out clean.
Cool to warm, about 15 minutes, before serving.

1 9" cheesecake pan or 1 12" tart flan pan. Serves 8

RISO E ZUCCA

Maria Belmonte, Caffe Portofino

1 medium sized onion
1 carrot
1 celery stalk
1 slice fatty bacon
2 tablespoons butter
1 pound pumpkin

Salt
4 cups meat broth
1¼ cup rice
1 scant cup grated Parmesan
    cheese

Chop the onion, carrot, celery and bacon. Put those chopped ingredients into a pot in which the butter has been melted and brown over a low flame for 10 minutes. Pass the bacon mixture through a food mill. Peel the pumpkin and cut into small cubes. Add the pieces of pumpkin to the bacon mixture and simmer for a time. Add salt and then the meat broth. Simmer over a low flame for 15 minutes. Add the rice and cook for about 15 minutes or until the rice is tender. Before serving, sprinkle with the Parmesan and stir vigorously.

Yield: Serves 4

POLENTA CASSEROLE
WITH SONOMA TELEME

David Viviani, Sonoma Cheese Factory

3 quarts chicken broth (reduce
    broth if thicker polenta is
    desired)
1½ tablespoons salt
3 cups polenta
½ cube butter

2 cups (approximately) your
    favorite spaghetti sauce
Grated Parmesan cheese or
    Sonoma Dry Jack
1 pound Sonoma Teleme
    cheese, sliced

Bring broth to a boil, add salt. Measure polenta into a bowl and add gradually into broth. Stir constantly. Turn heat down and continue stirring frequently for 50 minutes. Butter a shallow casserole dish and spread half the polenta in bottom. Put spaghetti sauce and cheese over this, then spread another layer of polenta, again topping with sauce and cheese. Use slices of Sonoma Teleme cheese between the layers. Bake in 375 degree oven for 30 minutes

Yield: 6 to 8 servings

PAELLA

Gloria Ferrer

Olive oil to cover the pan
2 cloves of garlic, not peeled
1 pound meat (chicken, sausage, pork, etc., or a mixture of all three)

½ red or green bell pepper in long slices
3 tablespoons tomato sauce or 1 small tomato, diced
8 threads of saffron
⅓ pound clean squid

Let everything brown evenly. When done add:

6-8 clams   1 cup rice

Mix everything well together and don't use spoon anymore. Add:

Handful of green peas
⅓ pound prawns, peeled
2½ cups (twice the amount of rice plus ½ cup more) of broth made from prawn shells, 4 more threads of saffron and 1 tablespoon of salt, boiling.

7-9 mussels pinched into the rice

Cook on stove for 7 minutes, lower heat and cook 5 more minutes or until rice is tender (transparent). If needed, add more broth. Steam covered with a paper bag for 5 more minutes. Can be decorated with roasted green or red pepper.

4 servings

SPICY PLUM SAUCE PORK, CHICKEN OR BEEF

Gary Chu's Gourmet Chinese Cuisine

¼ pound lean meat, cut into bite size (1 inch) pieces
½ bell pepper cut to desired size
1 leaf cabbage cut to desired size
6 slices carrot

6 thin slices black mushrooms
2 tablespoons white wine
3 tablespoons plum sauce
1 tablespoon soy bean
½ tablespoon chili paste
2 cloves garlic, pressed

Marinate the meat in one egg white and two teaspoons white wine. Heat the wok on high; when hot, add 12 ounces of vegetable oil. When the oil becomes warm, stir fry the marinated meat for 15 to 20 seconds or until meat is medium-rare. Leave the meat in wok, add vegetables and stir fry all for 10 seconds. Remove all from the wok and drain in metal colander. Wipe out the wok. Stir the garlic in wok for 5 seconds. Add plum sauce, soy bean paste and chili paste and mix well in the wok. Add the meats and vegetables and stir fry well. Add two teaspoons of sesame oil and stir. Serve with a shake of sesame seeds on top.

Soy bean paste and chili paste can be found in any Chinese grocery store.

FRUIT SMOOTHIE

National Dairy Council

½ cup plain yogurt
½ cup diced fruit such as banana, peach or strawberries

1-2 ice cubes

Place ingredients in a blender and purée until smooth.

Simi Winery

Simi is one of California's oldest and most respected wineries. Founded in 1876 by two Italian brothers from Tuscany, the winery is now under the French ownership of Moet-Hennessy/Louis Vuitton.

Simi is dedicated to making the highest quality wines; delicious, classic varietals that each have exceptional balance and finesse and express the vineyard's personality with complex aromas, intense flavors and supple, silky texture in the mouth.

Located in the heart of Sonoma County, Simi Winery welcomes visitors every day except Thanksgiving, Christmas, New Year's and Easter. One of the best ways to learn about the fine winemaking process is to take a scheduled tour at 11, 1 or 3 o'clock. Simi's resident chef also presents 12 food-and-wine pairing dinners and luncheons each year by reservation. Call for additional information.

16275 Healdsburg Avenue
Healdsburg, CA 95448
707-433-6981

Glen Ellen Winery

made its reputation producing premium varietal wines at affordable prices. The winery's Chardonnay, Merlot, Cabernet Sauvignon and White Zinfandel are consistently among the nation's top three sellers in their class.

Glen Ellen Winery is one of the wine country's premier visitor destinations, featuring a tasting room, a history center, and a gift shop. Located in historic Jack London Village, the winery is next door to the charms of fabled Glen Ellen.

The history center displays original photos and collectibles from the town of Glen Ellen in its heyday, while the Jack London Village features a number of artisans' shops.

Visitors can sample wines at the new tasting room in an 1881 winery. Tasting room hours: 10-5 daily.

Glen Ellen Winery
14301 Arnold Drive
Glen Ellen, CA 95442
(707) 939-6277

Rocky the Range Chicken

and his partner, Rocky Junior, are the most tender, juicy, succulent, flavorful chickens you can get. Produced exclusively by Petaluma Poultry Processors in the fertile, rolling hills of Petaluma, Rocky is raised on a vegetarian diet without antibiotics, raised longer than conventional birds, and is a true range chicken, with room to roam and forage. Wide open spaces, the good life, and a healthful diet has made Rocky the choice of discerning cooks.

Petaluma Poultry
    Processors, Inc.
P.O. Box 7368
Petaluma, CA 94955
707-763-1904

Redwood Hill Farm

Since 1968 our Redwood Hill Farm has been producing the finest-tasting goat milk products available. Our award-winning milk and yogurt are available at most Bay Area health and natural food outlets. Our delicious goat milk cheeses, including fresh chevre, feta, cheddar, smoked cheddar and "Camellia," a camembert-style cheese, are served at fine restaurants and are available at local retail outlets. Call for more information.

10855 Occidental Road
Sebastopol, CA 95472
707-823-8250

With each of our award-winning wines, De Loach Vineyards strives for consistency of style and excellence in quality year after year. From Chardonnay to Zinfandel, our wines are refined and balanced, each enhancing the meal with which it is served. We invite you to visit us at the winery.

Open 10:00 am - 4:30 pm
daily
1791 Olivet Road
Santa Rosa, CA 95401
(707) 526-9111

California Gold Dairy Products

California Cooperative Creamery has been a vital part of Sonoma County's agricultural community for more than 80 years. Doing business as California Gold Dairy Products, it represents superior quality milk and a variety of high quality, award winning cheese, butter and related dairy products. The Creamery continually receives awards for their own brand, California Gold, and other private labels.

The quality of California Gold's manufactured products is a result of the quality of milk produced in Sonoma County, among the highest in the country. Our dairy families say they have happy cows. A visit to dairy country will show why.

621 Western Ave.
Petaluma, CA 94952
(707) 763-1931

Gloria Ferrer
Champagne Caves

For over 100 years the Ferrer family of Spain has been producing *methode champenoise* sparkling wines, owning and operating seven wineries around the world. In 1982 Jose and Gloria Ferrer traveled from Barcelona, Catalonia to California in search of a microclimate and soil where Chardonnay and Pinot Noir would thrive. Their dreams led them to the Carneros Region of Sonoma where they built the first sparkling wine house in 1986. In just ten years Gloria Ferrer Champagne Caves has established itself as a top California sparkling wine producer with its many harvesting honors and world-wide acclaim for their sparkling wines, as well as the fourth vintage of world-class Estate Chardonnay and Pinot Noir wines. Salud!

23555 Casrneros Hwy. 121
Sonoma, CA 95476
707-996-7256
707-996-0720 (fax)

Santa Rosa
Meat and Poultry Co. Inc.

is a family owned and operated meat and poultry distributor. Specializing in quality and service, this U.S.D.A. inspected company offers a full line of the finest beef, pork, lamb and poultry products. They supply many restaurants, meat shops, delicatessens and caterers in the greater North Bay. Make sure the food you serve has come from the place where quality and service is everything.

940 Ludwig Avenue
Santa Rosa, CA 95402
(707) 542-6234

Petaluma Coffee Company,

quietly tucked away in Petaluma's historic river area at Foundry Wharf, offers a variety of coffees, teas, espresso drinks, fresh juices, light lunches and desserts. Watch master coffee roasters at work in this charming, eclectic atmosphere. Choose from a large selection of gourmet coffees, teas and accessories. For retail, wholesale or mail order call (800) 929-JAVA. We'll ship UPS.

189 H Street
Petaluma, CA 94952
707-763-2727

DESSERTS

APPLE-N-BLUEBERRY CRUMB PIE

Kozlowski Farms

Prepare a basic pie crust for bottom layer. Place in a deep dish 8 inch or 9 inch pie pan.

FILLING:

1 quart (approximately 5 large) sliced Gravenstein apples
1½ cups fresh or frozen blueberries
1½ cups sugar

2 tablespoons melted, unsalted butter
Dash of salt (approximately ½ teaspoon)
2 tablespoons tapioca

Fold together and place in pie crust

CRUMB TOPPING:

½ cup white sugar
½ cup flour
½ cup unsalted butter, softened

1 teaspoon cinnamon
1 cup pecans, finely chopped

Mix all ingredients together thoroughly until crumbly. Crumb pieces should not be too large. Crumble desired amount of topping on top of fruit mixture, and gently pat down. Bake in a 350 degree oven for 50 to 60 minutes. Serve with vanilla ice cream.

CRÈME ANGLAISE

Chef Thomas Oden, Jordan Winery

Heat 2 cups of milk with ½ cup of sugar until sugar dissolves. Pour a little of the hot milk mixture into a bowl with five slightly beaten egg yolks, stirring as you add it. Pour this mix back into the pot with the hot milk and slowly cook it, continuously stirring with a wooden spoon. When the cream starts to thinly coat the back of the spoon it is done. Strain into a chilled container, add vanilla extract to taste, and refrigerate until cold.

FRESH RED RASPBERRY CAKE

Kozlowski Farms

3 pounds (6 cups) fresh or frozen red raspberries with juice

2½ cups plus ¼ cup granulated sugar
3 loaves sweet French bread
1 pound butter (4 cubes)

Butter 9 inch springform pan and sprinkle ⅛ cup sugar on bottom and sides of pan. Blend raspberries and 2½ cups sugar together and set aside. Remove crust from French bread and slice in ½ inch thick slices. Butter each slice of bread on one side. Place slices butter side down on bottom and along sides of pan, making sure not to leave any holes. Now butter opposite side (top) of bread. Place 3 cups of raspberries on bread crust. Repeat another layer of bread using same butter process. Add the remaining 3 cups of berries and top with another layer of buttered bread. Butter top of crust and sprinkle with remaining ⅛ cup of sugar. Place a piece of plastic wrap on top of cake. Place a weighted plate on top of plastic wrap. Refrigerate overnight. Unmold cake pan, removing sides and bottom with sharp knife. Serve with whipped cream.

PAN DI SPAGNA

Chef Michael Ghilarducci, The Depot Hotel Restaurant and Italian Garden

4 eggs, separated
2 cups powdered sugar
Grated rind of one lemon
1 cup flour

Butter
Flour
Pinch of cream of tartar

Beat the egg whites until stiff with the cream of tartar. Refrigerate. Beat the yolks, add the powdered sugar and beat until thick and almost white. Fold in the lemon peel and then fold in the whites. Top with sifted flour and fold gently. When smooth, pour into a well-buttered and floured 9 inch pan and bake at 350 degrees for 30 minutes. Cool ten minutes in the pan and then one hour on the rack. Chill or freeze before slicing.

RASPBERRY COBBLER
FROM KOZLOWSKI FARMS

Kozlowski Farms

COBBLER DOUGH:

2½ cups sifted flour
1 tablespoon baking powder
1 teaspoon salt
½ cup sugar

1 cube unsalted butter,
  softened
¾ cup whole milk

COBBLER INGREDIENTS:

9 cups fresh or frozen red
  raspberries
1½ cups sugar

2 tablespoons fresh lemon
  juice
1 tablespoon tapioca

Combine all cobbler ingredients and place in a buttered baking dish. Set aside while preparing cobbler dough.

For Dough: Sift together all dry ingredients. With a pastry blender cut butter into all dry ingredients. When well blended add milk and gently mix with wooden spoon.

Arrange cobbler dough over red raspberries and bake in a 350 degree oven for approximately 1 hour or until golden brown. Let cool completely before serving.

Serving suggestion: Serve over ice cream topped with a fresh raspberry purée.

6-8 servings

Kozlowski Farms – Forestville

Packeeun '96

147

CARMEN KOZLOWSKI'S RASPBERRY BREAD

Kozlowski Farms

This was made in Carmen's Kitchen with Julia Child during a segment of "Good Morning America".

1 cup butter	½ cup buttermilk
1 cup sugar	3 cups flour
1 teaspoon vanilla	½ teaspoon salt
4 eggs	1 teaspoon cream of tartar
1 cup Kozlowski Farms Red Raspberry Jam	1 teaspoon baking soda

Cream butter, sugar and vanilla together. Add eggs, one at a time, beating well after each addition. Mix the dry ingredients and add alternately with the buttermilk. Marble in the raspberry jam. Pour into 2 greased and floured loaf pans. Bake at 325 degrees for 40 minutes or until done. (Bread should spring back when touched lightly in the center.)

2 loaves

INDIVIDUAL NECTARINE-RASPBERRY TARTS

Corey Basso, Le Bistro

1 cup flour	Nectarines
⅓ cup shortening	Raspberries
Cold water	

Cut flour and shortening together with pastry cutter until crumbly. Add cold water little by little blending with fork until dough forms a ball. Cut dough into 4 equal pieces. Roll out to 6 inch circles. Remove pit from nectarines and cut into thin wedges. Fan in circle on each dough, leaving about ½ inch to edge. Sprinkle with sugar. Wash raspberries lightly and mound in middle of tart. Sprinkle with more sugar. Pull edge of tart over fruit to encase it. Bake at 375 degrees for 10 to 15 minutes. Top each tart with vanilla ice cream and whipped cream.

4 servings

POACHED PEARS WITH KENDALL-JACKSON ZINFANDEL GLAZE

Chef Brian Leonard, La Crema Winery

There is a wide variety of pears available in Sonoma county and favorite is the Bosc variety from the Sebastopol area of Sonoma County. For this recipe I prefer using pears that are still slightly hard and underripe as they hold their shape and stand up better to the poaching process. Should Bosc pears be unavailable, use any variety of sweet, firm pear such as d'Anjou or Bartlett, also available from local farms. Make sure the apple juice you use is filtered, as unfiltered juice will yield a cloudy glaze. Instead of serving the pears and their glaze warm, this dish also is delicious chilled.

6 Bosc pears
3 cups Kendall-Jackson
   Vintner's Reserve Zinfandel

4 cups apple juice (filtered)
1 pinch cinnamon
1 pinch allspice

Peel and core the pears, leaving the stems intact. Heat the wine and apple juice in a medium-heavy stock pot over medium-high heat. Bring the mixture to a boil and add the pears to the pot. Reduce the heat to a simmer and cook the pears uncovered until soft when pierced, about 12 to 15 minutes. Gently remove the pears from the pot and set aside.

Bring the poaching liquid to a boil over high heat and cook until reduced to a syrup-like glaze, about 10 to 15 minutes. Place the pears on 6 dessert dishes and drizzle with the Zinfandel Glaze before serving.

Yield: 6 servings

SEMIFREDDO

Chef Thomas Oden, Jordan Winery

BASE RECIPE:

4 large egg yolks
½ cup (4 ounces) granulated
  sugar
3 large egg whites, beaten
  until stiff

1 cup (8 ounces) whipping
  cream, beaten until very
  thick

Beat the yolks and the sugar together until a thick ribbon forms. Fold in the flavoring until well incorporated. Fold in the egg whites. Fold in the whipped cream. Add any one of the following flavorings and pour into a dessert mold and freeze. Or, triple the recipe and make each of the three flavors and pour them into a long mold in layers, either symmetrically or abstractly, allowing each layer to set a bit before adding the next. When well frozen, slice into portions that reveal the layers. Serve with crème anglaise and butter cookies.

30 ounces

COFFEE:

3 ounces strong espresso

1 ounce coffee liqueur

Combine and cool.

PISTACHIO:

½ cup (4 ounces) pistachio
  nuts, skins removed as well
  as reasonably possible

2 ounces granulated sugar

In a non-stick pan heat the nuts and sugar over moderate heat to melt and lightly caramelize the sugar as well as toast the nuts. Pour out when done, allow to cool, break into chunks and grind in a food processor with a pulsing action until the form of a corn meal texture. A range of grain size is good.

CHOCOLATE:

2 ounces of bittersweet
  chocolate

½ ounce rum
½ ounce of whipping cream

Melt chocolate over hot water. Add rum and cream. Cool.

4 servings

TIRAMISU

Chef Michael Ghilarducci, The Depot Hotel Restaurant and
Italian Garden

One "Pan di Spagna" cake, cooled or frozen (recipe on p. 145)
25 ounces Mascarpone cheese
1½ cups heavy cream
½ box powdered sugar
½ cup rum
1½ teaspoon vanilla
2 cups espresso
Additional rum

8 ounces grated dark high-
quality chocolate
1 cup heavy cream sweetened
and whipped, for garnish
8 chocolate covered espresso
beans, for garnish

Bake the Pan di Spagna sponge cake, chill and slice in half once
horizontally. Make espresso and reserve. In a large mixing bowl
beat Mascarpone, heavy cream, powdered sugar, ½ cup rum and
vanilla until it forms a soft peak. Using a pastry brush spread the
espresso on the cake layers and then sprinkle with the additional
rum. On one layer of cake spread half the Mascarpone mixture
and then sprinkle liberally with half of the grated chocolate.
Place the second layer on top and repeat with a layer of
Mascarpone and then the grated chocolate. Wrap in plastic
and refrigerate until ready to serve, at least two hours. To
serve, pipe on whipped cream and garnish with chocolate-
covered espresso beans.

8 servings

GINGER CRÈME BRÛLÉE

Mary Evely, Chef, Simi Winery

1 quart whipping cream
2 inch piece fresh ginger
8 large egg yolks

½ cup granulated sugar plus
¼ cup additional for
caramelizing

Peel ginger and slice into ⅟₁₆ inch thick coins. Put into saucepan with the cream and heat until just about to boil. Remove from heat and let steep for 10 minutes. Preheat oven to 325 degrees. Beat the egg yolks and ½ cup sugar until thick and pale yellow. Add the cream (in small increments at first), stirring to incorporate. Strain. Skim off foam which may form on top of the mixture, then pour into eight 6 ounce custard cups. Place cups in a baking pan half filled with warm water. Lay a sheet of waxed paper over the cups and bake 45 to 55 minutes, until custard begins to set. Remove from water bath and chill until set. To serve, cover tops of custards with a thin layer of sugar** and caramelize with a blow torch* until nicely browned. Place brûlées on saucers and serve immediately, taking care not to touch the edges of the cups, which will be very hot.

Small propane blow torches are available at a reasonable price at most hardware stores. They are very easy to operate, and are truly the easiest way to caramelize the sugar without melting the custard.

**I prefer the flavor of brown sugar for the caramelizing. If you wish to try it, you need to dry out the sugar in the oven and repulverize it, as it otherwise has too much moisture to caramelize properly.*

SPICED PRALINE CHEESE CAKE

Chef Phil McGauley, Korbel Winery

CRUST:

1 cup graham cracker crumbs   ¼ cup butter, melted

FILLING:

1½ pound cream cheese   1 cup pecans, chopped
1¼ cups brown sugar, finely   2 tablespoons flour
   packed   2 tablespoons Korbel Spiced
3 eggs   Brandy

TOPPING:

½ cup brown sugar, firmly   1 tablespoon Korbel Spiced
   packed   Brandy
¼ cup butter

For crust: Combine crumbs and butter in large bowl and mix well. Press evenly in bottom of 9 inch springform pan.

For filling: Preheat oven to 350 degrees. Blend cheese and 1¼ cup brown sugar in bowl until smooth. Add eggs one at a time, beating well after each addition. Stir in pecans, flour and spiced brandy and mix thoroughly. Pour into prepared pan, spreading evenly. Bake until set, 50 to 55 minutes. Let cheesecake cool to room temperature, then cover and refrigerate overnight.

For topping: Combine brown sugar and butter in saucepan. Place over low heat and cook, stirring occasionally, until smooth and thickened, about 5 minutes. Pour hot topping over chilled cheesecake, spreading to cover top. Remove springform. Arrange pecans decoratively around edge of topping. Serve cheesecake slightly chilled or at room temperature with your favorite fruit sauce.

6-8 servings

OLIVE OIL AND CHARDONNAY CAKE WITH DRIED FRUIT COMPOTE AND PINOT NOIR SYRUP

Chef Brian Leonard, La Crema Winery

With the delicious, high quality olive oils now being made locally, I developed this cake which instead of using the usual butter, incorporates olive oil, a more heart-healthy monounsaturated fat. When baking this cake, do not be alarmed when it deflates during baking. This is meant to happen and in the end you will have a dense, rich dessert. The dried lavender blossoms and Chardonnay add a floral complexity to the cake which compliments the Dried Fruit Compote accompaniment. The Dried Fruit Compote and Syrup also make a delicious topping for vanilla ice cream.

3 large egg yolks
⅓ cup plus 1 tablespoon extra fine sugar
½ tablespoon fresh lemon zest
½ cup all purpose flour
¼ teaspoon salt

1 teaspoon dried lavender blossoms
¼ cup La Crema Chardonnay
¼ cup plus 1 tablespoon extra virgin olive oil
5 large egg whites at room temperature.

Preheat oven to 375 degrees. Butter and lightly flour one 9-inch pan and set aside.

Place the egg yolks, sugar and lemon zest in a large stainless steel bowl and place directly over a low flame for 30 seconds, beating constantly with a wire whisk. Remove the bowl from the heat and continue beating with an electric mixer until the bottom of the bowl is cool to the touch and the mixture thickens and triples in volume, about 5 to 8 minutes. Sift the flour and salt together into a separate bowl. Gradually add the flour to the egg yolk mixture, beating constantly until a thick paste is formed and the flour is incorporated.

Place the egg whites in a clean bowl and whip to soft peaks. (Note: If using an electric mixer, make sure the beaters are clean without a trace of oil or egg yolk, as these will prohibit the whites from completely rising.) Slowly add the lavender, Chardonnay and olive oil to the egg yolk mixture, then gently fold in the whipped egg whites in 3 stages, being careful not to overmix or deflate the batter. Pour the cake batter into the prepared pan. Place the pan on the middle rack of the oven and bake at 375 degrees for 15 minutes. Lower the temperature to 275 degrees and continue baking until the cake is brown and a tester inserted into the middle comes out clean, about 15 to 20 minutes.

Remove the cake from the oven and allow to cool in the pan for at least 30 minutes before serving. Slice the cake into 8 servings and top with Dried Fruit Compote, spooning the Pinot Noir syrup over each portion.

8 servings

DRIED FRUIT COMPOTE
WITH PINOT NOIR SYRUP

Chef Brian Leonard, La Crema Winery

3 cups La Crema Pinot Noir   ½ cup cranberries
½ cup dried figs   ½ cup dried cherries
½ cup dried apricots   1 crushed juniper berry

Place the wine in a large, heavy saucepan over medium-high heat and bring to a low boil. Add the fruit and juniper berry to the pan and lower the heat to a simmer. Cook the fruit until it is reconstituted and plump, about 15 to 20 minutes. Reserving the fruit, strain the wine into a clean saucepan, and return to a medium boil over high heat until reduced to a syrup.

Serve the Dried Fruit Compote and Pinot Noir syrup with the Olive Oil and Chardonnay Cake.

Yield: 3 cups

CHOCOLATE RUM PARFAIT

Chef Robert Buchschachermaier, Cafe Europe

5 ounces sugar
3 eggs
4 egg yolks
dash salt
1 teaspoon vanilla sugar
3 tablespoons rum

4 ounces water
2 ounces cocoa powder
5 ounces Belgian or
    Hershey's chocolate
    (baking chocolate)
½ liter heavy cream

Bring water and cocoa powder to boiling point. Put aside and add the chocolate. Add rum. Use a whip to smoothen the paste. Let it cool. Whip heavy cream and put it in the refrigerator. Bring water in a large pot (½ full) to boil. Using a large bowl (which fits over the pot) add eggs, sugar, yolks, vanilla sugar and a dash of salt. Place over the boiling water. Using a medium sized whip, start beating until it is creamy and about three times the amount from start. Keep moving the bowl and be careful so the mixture does not curdle. Remove from stove and place bowl over ice water. Keep beating until the cream is cold. To the cold mixture add the chocolate rum paste. Slowly fold the whipped cream under. Fill in paper cups. Cover with food wrap and place in freezer for 12 hours. Serve with raspberry sauce, whipped cream and cookies.

4 servings

RASPBERRY SAUCE

Chef Robert Buchschachermaier, Cafe Europe

12 ounces frozen raspberries,
    thawed to room
    temperature

2 tablespoons sugar
3 tablespoons cognac

Purée raspberries in a food processor, the force through a fine sieve to strain out seeds. Stir in sugar and cognac. Refrigerate.

1 cup

ORANGE CRÊPE WITH A SUMMER FRUIT COMPOTE

Michael Valmassoi, Center City Diner

CRÊPE:

½ cup flour
1 egg
½ cup milk
1 orange, zest

2 tablespoons sugar
1 egg white
¼ cup orange juice

Mix flour and sugar. Add eggs, milk, orange juice and stir until smooth. Let sit for one hour. To cook, thinly coat nonstick egg pan with butter. Cook until just golden then turn out crêpe and fold into a triangle. Repeat.

FRUIT COMPOTE:

Toss together sliced apricots, peaches, strawberries, blackberries, ollalieberries, mission figs and a little sugar. Allow to macerate for a few hours. To serve, spoon macerated fruit into bowl. Fill crêpe with fresh whipped cream. Place on top of berries. Dust with powdered sugar and serve.

4 servings

GOAT CHEESE TART

Patty Salmon, Bodega Goat Cheese

16 ounces Queso Ranchero,
    plain or no salt
3 eggs
1 can evaporated goat milk
    (12 ounces)

1 cup sugar
8 ounces goat milk
5 slices of whole wheat bread
    (crust removed)

Mix on low flame, sugar and evaporated milk until it thickens slightly. Mix cheese, eggs and goat milk with hand mixer for 2 minutes until well blended. Add bread, mashing with mixture until it is well blended. Put in a greased baking mold. Bake at 350 degrees for about an hour until brown on top. Top with apricot jam, fresh berries and/or fruit slices.

SINFULLY LIGHT CHEESECAKE

California Milk Advisory Board

A luscious, creamy cheesecake at only 240 calories per slice. Topped with a moist fresh fruit topping, add another 15 calories per slice.

CRUST:

1 cup graham cracker crumbs   2 tablespoons melted butter

FILLING:

¾ cup sugar
½ teaspoon <u>each</u> grated orange and lemon rind
2 tablespoons all-purpose flour

2 pounds part skim ricotta cheese
2 teaspoons vanilla
4 eggs
dash salt

Combine crust ingredients in bottom of lightly buttered 8 or 9 inch springform pan. Press onto bottom only; crust will be crumbly. Combine filling ingredients in food processor, or beat together until smooth. Pour onto prepared crust. Put springform pan into roasting pan. Pour hot water in roasting pan halfway up sides of springform pan. This will help keep cheese-cake moist. Bake in 375 degree oven for 55 minutes to 1 hour, or until top is just set. Cool and chill for at least 1 hour before serving.

12 servings

USES FOR YOGURT IN DESSERTS

National Dairy Council

Combine plain yogurt with powdered sugar to taste and spread on brownies. Sprinkle on shaved chocolate and bake 5 minutes in a 350 degree oven for a creamy glaze.

Fold green seedless grapes into plain yogurt and chill at least 1 hour. Serve, sprinkled with brown sugar.

CRAZY CHOCO-RAZZLEBERRY CAKE

Carol Shelton, Windsor Vineyards

This recipe is an old family favorite from our winemaker, Carol Shelton. She calls it "Crazy Cake" because it has no eggs, but it does have vinegar!

3 cups flour
2 cups sugar
2 teaspoons baking soda
1 teaspoon salt
6 tablespoons cocoa
2 cups cold water

10 tablespoons melted butter
or margarine
2 tablespoons raspberry
vinegar
2 teaspoons vanilla
1-2 cups fresh raspberries
(optional)

Preheat oven to 325 degrees. Sift together all dry ingredients except cocoa. Dissolve cocoa in some of the cold water. Make a hole in the middle of the dry ingredients in the mixing bowl and pour all liquid ingredients into the hole. Mix well with mixer. Gently fold in raspberries if desired and in season. Pour into 13 x 9 x 2 inch pan or two 9 inch round cake pans and bake for 35-45 minutes, until toothpick comes out clean at the center. If you do the 2-layer cake format, definitely put fresh raspberries in the icing (see following recipe) between the layers and decorate the top of the cake with more berries.

Yield: Serves 8

CHOCO-RAZZLEBERRY ICING

Carol Shelton, Windsor Vineyards

1 ounce bitter baking
chocolate, melted
3 tablespoons butter or
margarine
1½ cups confectioner's sugar,
sifted

pinch salt
1 teaspoon vanilla
½ cup no-sugar-added
raspberry jam.

Cream sugar and shortening and slowly beat in the melted chocolate, then the salt, jam and vanilla. Be conservative on the sugar addition until the jam is in, since it's going to add sweetness. Adjust to your own taste with confectioner's sugar.

You'll need to double the above amounts if you are making a layered cake versus a pan cake.

WALNUT ORANGE TART

Jeffrey Madura, John Ash and Company

FOR THE CRUST:

1 cup flour
½ cup butter, chilled and
    diced small

1 teaspoon vanilla
1-2 teaspoons ice water
    (if needed)

Quickly combine flour, butter and vanilla until dough resembles coarse oatmeal. If too dry, add drops of ice water. Gather into a ball, cover with plastic and chill for at least 30 minutes. Roll out dough to fit a 9 inch removable bottom tart pan. Prick dough well and bake for 6-7 minutes in a preheated 350 degree oven until crust is set and very lightly browned. Cool.

FOR THE FILLING:

¾ cup cream
¾ cup sugar
1 tablespoon zest from one
    medium orange
½ teaspoon vanilla

Big pinch of salt
2 tablespoons Grand Marnier
    or other orange brandy
1½ cups whole walnuts

Heat sugar and cream in a sauce pan until it just simmers and the mixture becomes translucent. Stir in the zest, vanilla salt and brandy. Fill shell with an even layer of walnuts and pour the cream mixture over. Place tart on a baking sheet and bake for 30-35 minutes at 350 degrees. Tart should be lightly browned on top. It will bubble as it bakes. Cool and serve warm or at room temperature. Do not refrigerate. Garnish with fresh berries and a little crème anglaise or lightly sweetened whipped cream.

Yield: Serves 8

WHITE NECTARINES POACHED IN **J** WITH FENNEL MASCARPONE CREAM

Chef Thomas Oden, Jordan Winery

POACHED NECTARINES:

2 pounds white nectarines   ½ cup sugar
2 cups J, Jordan Sparkling
    Wine

In a non-corroding saucepan, simmer 1½ cups of the J with the sugar for 5 minutes. Slice the nectarines in half, pit and peel. Cut the halves in ¾ inch slices and, depending on their ripeness, cook for 4 to 6 minutes in the wine syrup. Chill the nectarines in their syrup. Drain the nectarines, reserving the syrup and mixing it with the remaining ½ cup of J.

FENNEL MASCARPONE CREAM:

1 egg yolk   1 tablespoon Sambuca, or
1 tablespoon sugar   other anise-flavored liqueur
½ cup J, Jordan Sparkling   ½ cup mascarpone
    Wine

In a bowl over boiling water, beat the egg yolk with the J and the sugar until it mounts into a zabaglione. Add the Sambuca and cool the bowl rapidly in a bath of ice water. Fold in the mascarpone and chill until ready to serve.

Serve the fruit in a sherbet cup or margarita glass topped with some of the syrup, a dollop of the fennel cream and a sprig of mint. If desired, serve a simple butter cookie on the side.

Yield: Serves 4

ARMIDA MERLOT TRUFFLES

Kathy Cousins-Starkey, Armida Winery, Healdsburg

FOR TRUFFLE CENTERS:

10 ounces semisweet or bittersweet chocolate, cut into bits

3 tablespoons sweet butter, cut into bits
1 cup heavy cream
½ cup Armida Merlot

FOR DIPPING:

2 pounds semisweet or bittersweet chocolate, cut into bits

TO MAKE TRUFFLE MIXTURE:

Place chocolate and butter in a medium bowl, set aside. In a saucepan, bring cream to a simmer. Remove from heat and pour over chocolate and butter. Stir gently until chocolate is completely melted and mixture is smooth. Stir in Armida Merlot. Strain mixture into another bowl. Let cool without stirring. Refrigerate until very firm, at least 4 hours.

TO FORM CENTERS:

Scrape a spoon across the surface of the cold truffle mixture and form 1 inch balls. Place balls on a pan and freeze for several hours or overnight.

TO DIP CENTER:

Melt chocolate in a clean dry medium bowl set in a pan of barely simmering water. Stir frequently. When chocolate is smooth and melted and about 115° to 120°, remove from water bath. Pour chocolate into a clean shallow pan. Dip the truffle centers into the melted chocolate until entirely coated. Place coated truffles on paper-lined cookie sheet. Place tray of dipped truffles in refrigerator to set coating. Once coating has set, remove truffles from paper and they are ready to eat.

About 2 dozen large truffles.

Kozlowski Farms Sonoma County Classics

For more than 35 years, visitors have journeyed to the landmark Kozlowski Farms Store and apple ranch to experience the wholesome goodness of their organic fruit and natural gourmet food products. What began as a raspberry farm with a tiny fruit stand is today an acclaimed operation boasting sales throughout the U.S., Canada, Europe and the Far East.

Kozlowski Farms is a family owned and operated business presided over by founder Carmen and her three children, Carol, Perry and Cindy. All recipes for their products are conceived in the Kozlowski kitchens and produced at the farm.

Kozlowski Farms has also become known for their award-winning gift baskets. The most recent honor: Best of Show at the 1996 Sonoma County Harvest Fair. (Second year in a row.)

The Farm Store itself is an excellent visitor destination, featuring a tasting room where all 50-plus Kozlowski Farms gourmet products are available for sampling. In addition to the tasting room, guests can enjoy homemade delicacies from the bakery and deli. Large picnic grounds offer a breathtaking view of the surrounding valley.

Visitors to Sonoma County are warmly welcomed at the Farm Store and Tasting Room by family members and Sam, the farm cat. Kozlowski Farms Store and Tasting Room is open to the public daily year round. Call or write for their free mail order catalogue and gold-medal recipes.

5566 Gravenstein Highway No.
Forestville, CA 95436
707-887-1587
707-887-9650 (fax)

Armida Winery

has long been known for producing superior quality wines. A tradition of showcasing Russian River Valley varietals by enhancing their characteristics was begun by winemaker Frank Churchill when Armida first opened and continues under Frank's gentle hand today. Our winery setting on Westside Road in Healdsburg offers one of the most spectacular views in all of Sonoma County. Oak trees estimated at 180 years old provide a canopy of dappled shade over our redwood deck. Relaxing with a glass of wine overlooking our bocce court and our flower-filled grounds has become a favorite pastime of locals and friends who come to visit. Include some of the finest foods and produce that Sonoma County has to offer and you have the perfect combination for a memorable wine country experience.

Armida Winery
2201 Westside Road
Healdsburg, CA 95448
707-433-2222

Art Ibleto, "The Pasta King"

Art is a sharing, caring person who loves to cook good food and give enjoyment to others. From minestrone to pesto, from polenta to lasagna, he knows how to make meals appealing and delicious.

He keeps a rigorous schedule of cooking for church and other charity fund-raisers at prices that allow these fund-raisers to be desirable as well as successful.

See Art in action at the Sonoma County Fair and the Farmer's Market – making pasta and polenta and selling prepared sauces. A true "son of Italy," Art's philosophy is "you do something good, people love it."

1492 Lowell Ave.
Cotati, CA 49431
707-792-2712

MENUS

Executive Chef Todd Muir
of Madrona Manor, and
Chef Proprietor of Mangia Bene

I have selected four recipes that announce the end of spring and the beginning of summer. These dishes have all been well received at Madrona Manor. The first course is a goat cheese timbale, a light, playful appetizer that lets the subtle flavor of the goat cheese shine. The fresh corn cakes served warm on a bed of Dungeness crab, the jewel of the Sonoma Coast, hails the beginning of summer for me. The entree, using rack of lamb, is a match made in heaven for almost any red wine. Last, but not least, chocolate taco brings this menu to a close on a playful note once again.

Poached pear and goat cheese timbale with sliced prosciutto, candied walnuts and raspberry vinaigrette

Corn cakes with crab salsa, sour cream and caviar

Sonoma County rack of lamb with honey glazed root vegetables, potato gâteau, and currant-marjoram sauce

Chocolate taco with chocolate mousse garnished with tropical fruit, coconut and raspberry sauce

POACHED PEAR AND GOAT CHEESE TIMBALE

GOAT CHEESE TIMBALE:
1 cup cream
3 eggs

2 ounces goat cheese
Salt and white pepper to taste

Mix cream and eggs. Season to taste. Spray small timbale with non-stick spray. Crumble cheese into timbale. Pour in cream and mix. Cook in water bath for 20 minutes in 350 degree oven or until set.

RASPBERRY VINAIGRETTE:
½ cup walnut oil
1 tablespoon raspberry vinegar
12 raspberries puréed
Salt and sugar to taste

1 teaspoon chopped mint
 leaves
1 egg yolk

In blender make dressing. Season to taste. Add chopped mint.

CANDIED WALNUTS:
½ cup walnuts
¼ cup powdered sugar

Vegetable oil for deep frying

Blanch walnuts in boiling water one minute. Toss walnuts in powdered sugar. Deep fry in small amounts. Be careful not to burn them! Place on sheet pan to cool

POACHED PEARS:
3 pears
1 bottle red wine
2 cups sugar

2 cinnamon sticks
1 vanilla bean

Peel and core pears. Add sugar, cinnamon sticks, and vanilla bean to red wine. Simmer and poach pears until tender but not soft, about 20 minutes. Cool in liquid.

TO SERVE:
Goat cheese timbale
Sliced prosciutto
Crumbled goat cheese

Poached pear
Candied walnuts
Bachelor button flowers
Mint sprig

Place two prosciutto slices in center of plate. Place timbale in center of prosciutto. Fan one-quarter pear on both sides of timbale. Drizzle vinaigrette. Crumble goat cheese around plate. Place walnuts around plate. Garnish with flowers and mint sprig.

CORN CAKES WITH CRAB SALSA, SOUR CREAM AND CAVIAR

CORN CAKES:

4 ears worth of corn kernels
1 tablespoon roasted bell
   pepper, sliced
1 egg

Salt and pepper to taste
1 teaspoon baking powder
½ cup masa flour

Grind corn kernels or chop coarse in food processor. Strain off some of the liquid or "milk". Add all other ingredients. Mix thoroughly. Fry in skillet with a small amount of oil on moderate heat. Turn over after a few minutes and cake is a nice brown color. Serve with crab salsa (see recipe below). Garnish with a dollop of sour cream and caviar.

CRAB SALSA:

½ cup crab meat
½ cup corn kernels, blanched
1 tablespoon cilantro, chopped
¼ red tomato, chopped
¼ yellow tomato, chopped

¼ orange tomato, chopped
½ lime or lemon, juiced
Salt to taste
A few strands saffron
¾ cup extra virgin olive oil

Mix all ingredients thoroughly. Makes 8 cakes.

RACK OF LAMB

Sonoma County rack of lamb with honey glazed root vegetables, potato gateau, and currant-marjoram sauce.

1 rack of lamb marinated
   three hours in:
2 tablespoons olive oil
1 tablespoon red wine

1 teaspoon garlic, chopped
1 tablespoon mixed fresh
   herbs, chopped
Salt and pepper to taste

Grill lamb to desired temperature.

WINTER VEGETABLES

2 turnips peeled, cut into
  wedges
2 rutabagas peeled, cut into
  wedges
1 carrot peeled, cut in ½ and
  then into wedges

2 parsnips peeled, cut into
  wedges
2 tablespoons butter
2 teaspoons mixed fresh herbs
  chopped
1 tablespoon honey
Salt and pepper to taste

Blanch all vegetables. Heat butter in sauté pan, add all ingredients and sauté a few minutes to get a light golden color. Serve hot. Serves 8

POTATO GÂTEAU

12 potatoes, peeled, sliced very
  thin
1 tablespoon chopped fresh
  herbs

Salt and pepper to taste
3 tablespoons clarified butter

Line a 12 inch x 3 inch x 2½ inch terrine mold with plastic wrap. Toss potatoes with rest of ingredients. Layer potatoes in mold to the top. Pour over butter. Cover with lid or aluminum foil. Bake in a 350 degree oven for 1 hour, 15 minutes. Remove from oven and weight down. Refrigerate overnight. To serve, unmold, slice down the middle and cut into 16 pieces. Heat in a 350 degree oven for 15 minutes. Serves 8.

CURRANT-MARJORAM SAUCE

1 cup reduced lamb stock
2 cups red wine

1 teaspoon chopped marjoram
2 tablespoons currants

Reduce all ingredients to desired consistency. Serve hot. Serves eight.

CHOCOLATE TACO
WITH CHOCOLATE MOUSSE
GARNISHED WITH TROPICAL FRUIT,
COCONUT AND RASPBERRY SAUCE

1 pound sugar
1 pound butter softened
16 egg whites

12 ounces flour
4 ounces cocoa powder

Mix all ingredients thoroughly. Spread a tablespoon of mix in an oblong circle. While still warm peel off pan and bend over a rolling pin. Cool. Fill with mousse and tropical fruit. Garnish with raspberry sauce and white chocolate curls.

CHOCOLATE MOUSSE:
13 ounces semisweet chocolate
7 egg whites
1/4 teaspoon cream of tartar

3 cups cream
1 1/2 teaspoons vanilla extract

Melt chocolate in a double boiler and cool to luke warm. In a large bowl beat the egg whites with cream of tartar to stiff peak stage but not dry. In another bowl beat cream with vanilla until stiff. Fold chocolate carefully into egg whites then into cream.

FILLING:
Chocolate mousse
Tropical fruit
Mango
Papaya
Pineapple

Strawberry
Whipped cream
White chocolate curls
Raspberry sauce
Coconut

Chef Proprietor Patrick Martin, Healdsburg Charcuterie

*Goat Cheese and Roasted Garlic Terrine
with Tomato Vinaigrette*

Ratatouille

*Cured Pork Tenderloin
with Pepper and
Tomato Relish*

Short Bread Crusted Cheese Cake

Restaurant Charcuterie – Healdsburg.

Pelham '96

GOAT CHEESE AND ROASTED GARLIC TERRINE WITH TOMATO VINAIGRETTE

GOAT CHEESE TERRINE:

3 cups heavy cream	4 ounces goat cheese
6 whole eggs	1 cup roasted garlic cloves
6 yolks	Salt and pepper to taste

Mix goat cheese and heavy cream until well blended. Mix eggs, yolks, salt and pepper and garlic. Add goat cheese mixture to eggs, mix well. Pour in a terrine 3 x 11 x 3 inches. Put terrine in a bain marie. Bake in a 375 degree oven for 45 to 60 minutes.

TOMATO VINAIGRETTE:

Yield: 2 cups

4 tomatoes, peeled, seeded and diced	1 tablespoon chives
	⅓ cup balsamic vinegar
½ cup chopped basil	Juice of 1 lemon
1 tablespoon chopped shallots	½ cup olive oil
1 tablespoon chopped parsley	Salt and pepper to taste

Combine all the ingredients. Let mixture marinate for at least 4 hours.

To Serve: Slice terrine about 1 inch thick and place on blanket of tomato vinaigrette. Garnish with long pieces of chive.

Yield: 8 servings

Tomato vinaigrette is excellent as a relish for fish too.

RATATOUILLE

¼ cup olive oil
2 medium sized yellow onions, chopped
4 medium sized eggplant, unpeeled and cut into 1 inch cubes
3 large green, red and/or yellow bell peppers, seeded, deribbed and cut into 1 inch pieces

2 tablespoons fresh thyme
1 bay leaf
3½-4 pounds tomatoes (10-12 medium sized), peeled and chopped
¼ cup minced fresh basil
1 head of garlic, peeled and chopped

In a large saucepan warm the olive oil and onions and sauté at low heat for about ½ hour or until onions are nice and golden. Add peppers and garlic, sauté for 5 minutes. Add the rest of the ingredients and cook at low heat uncovered for 1½ to 2 hours. Salt and pepper to taste.

Yield: 4 to 6 servings

Gets even better the next day. Excellent as side dish or main dish for lighter supper.

CURED PORK TENDERLOIN WITH PEPPER AND TOMATO RELISH

PORK TENDERLOIN:

¼ cup salt
½ cup sugar
2 quarts water

3 pork tenderloins (about 1 pound each)
Olive oil and butter

Mix together salt, sugar and water. Soak tenderloins overnight. Drain, rinse and pat dry. Brown in olive oil and butter in sauté pan or skillet until brown. Bake in 450 degree oven for 15 minutes. Serve with pepper and tomato relish.

This is an excellent method of curing pork. Pork chops cured in this method are also superb.

PEPPER AND TOMATO RELISH:

3 large tomatoes, peeled and seeded
3 bell peppers, roasted, peeled and minced
2 cloves garlic, minced

1 teaspoon cumin
¼ teaspoon cayenne
1 tablespoon lemon juice
¼ cup chopped parsley

Sauté tomatoes for 6 minutes or until dry. Add rest of ingredients. Mix well. Season with salt and pepper to taste. Serve at room temperature.

Yield: 6 servings

SHORT BREAD CRUSTED CHEESE CAKE

A wonderful light no-bake cheese cake.

CRUST:

4 ounces butter
½ cup powdered sugar
2 cups flour

½ cup chopped nuts (walnuts,
    almonds or pine nuts)

Blend as pie crust with pastry blender. Bake in greased pan for
8 to 10 minutes at 350 degrees.

FILLING:

Juice of ½ lemon
8 ounces cream cheese
¾ cup powdered sugar

1 teaspoon vanilla extract
1 cup cream, whipped

Mix cream cheese, sugar, lemon and vanilla. Fold in whipped cream.
Spread on chilled shortbread crust and chill at least six hours before
serving. Garnish pieces with fresh fruit or edible flowers.

Yield: 9 x 13 inch cake

MIXX, An American Bistro,
Proprietor Chef, Dan Berman

Oysters on the Half Shell
with Lemon-Vodka Mousseline and Caviar

Goat Cheese Tart

Sonoma Duck Breast
with Natural Juices,
Blackberry Merlot Purée and Arugula

Medallions of Lamb
with Sun-Dried Cranberries
and Pinot Noir

Cointreau Custard Tart

OYSTERS ON THE HALF SHELL WITH LEMON-VODKA MOUSSELINE AND CAVIAR

2 dozen oysters
1 ounce vodka
2 lemons, zest and juice

1 cup heavy cream
1 ounce caviar

In a well chilled bowl whisk together the cream, vodka and half the zest. Whip to soft peaks. Slowly add juice, whisking all the while. Whip back to soft peaks and fold in rest of zest.

Shuck oysters and carefully cut muscle from bottom of shell, where oyster attaches. Place oysters on rock salt, 6 oysters per plate with rock salt underneath. Place one small spoonful of Mousseline on top of oyster. Garnish with caviar and a sprig of parsley in center and serve immediately. Serve with chilled vodka or champagne.

GOAT CHEESE TART

CRUST:
1½ cups flour
¼ teaspoon salt
6 tablespoons butter

2 tablespoons Gorgonzola
¼ cup water (ice cold)

FILLING:
4 ounces ricotta cheese
8 ounces goat cheese
1 egg yolk
2 tablespoons chopped fresh
    herbs*

1 tablespoon flour
½ teaspoon coarse black
    pepper

Combine flour and salt in processor, pulse to combine. Add butter and Gorgonzola (chilled and cut into small pieces). Pulse to texture of course crumbs. Add water slowly through feed tube and process just until mixture forms a ball. Wrap and chill 3 to 4 hours. Roll ⅛ inch thick and place in tart or quiche pan. Pre-bake (with foil and weight) 10 minutes at 375 degree preheated oven. Remove foil and weight from crust and bake 10 to 15 minutes more until light brown. Cool before adding filling.

For filling combine ingredients and add to cooled shell. Bake in preheated 375 degree oven for 25 to 30 minutes.

*Robin used 1 tablespoon each basil and rosemary, any herbs are okay.

SONOMA DUCK BREAST WITH NATURAL JUICES, BLACKBERRY MERLOT PURÉE AND ARUGULA

SALAD:

½ red bell pepper, cut into ¼ inch beunoise or cube, pith and seeds removed.

1 cup jicama, peeled, cut into ¼ inch beunoise or cube

½ cup Sweet 100 red tomatoes, halved.

½ cup Sweet 100 gold tomatoes, halved.

½ cup golden beets, peeled and cut into ¼ inch beunoise or cube, blanch for 15 seconds

½ cup Blue Lake beans, cut into ¼ inch pieces, blanch for 30 seconds

½ cup Yukon Gold potatoes, cut into ¼ inch beunoise or cube, blanched until tender but firm, about 30 seconds in boiling water.

4 ounces stemmed arugula

Prepare all the vegetables ahead of time and toss in a bowl until evenly mixed. Set aside.

DRESSING:

1 tablespoon chopped shallots

1 tablespoon Dijon mustard

1½ tablespoons diced cooked applewood bacon

3 tablespoons rice wine vinegar

1 tablespoon Champagne vinegar

12 tablespoons extra virgin olive oil

Salt and fresh ground black pepper to taste

1 teaspoon chopped tarragon

In a mixing bowl, combine shallots, bacon, rice wine vinegar, Champagne vinegar and a pinch of salt. Whisk together. Add mustard and whisk again. Slowly add olive oil, whisking until incorporated. Add tarragon and season with salt and pepper. Set aside.

BLACKBERRY PURÉE: 2 ounces blackberry brandy
1 cup blackberries
¼ cup merlot

Purée blackberries with merlot and blackberry brandy. Strain through fine mesh strainer so there are no seeds. Get all the juice. Set aside.

DUCK:
6 half duck breasts (3 whole breasts)

Season each half breast lightly with salt and pepper. Lightly coat skillet with oil and heat until almost smoking. Duck breast should be cleaned so fat is about ⅛ inch to ¼ inch thick. Place duck in a skillet fat side down. Turn down heat to medium and sauté 3 minutes, shaking pan gently, until fat is golden brown. Turn over, pour off most of fat, and sauté 1½ to 2 minutes meat side down until well browned. Place skillet in preheated 350 degree oven, fat side down for 3 minutes, until medium rare. After 3 minutes remove skillet from oven, remove duck from skillet and place on plate. Keep warm and let rest for 3 to 4 minutes.

PRESENTATION:
On large round plates, divide arugula evenly in little beds at top of the plate. Toss dressing with vegetables and divide evenly on top of arugula. Build salad high. Fan duck breast and place on bottom of plate. Pour natural juices over duck using a squirt bottle or spoon, garnish with blackberry purée, not being excessive. Serve immediately.

6 servings.

MEDALLIONS OF LAMB
WITH SUN-DRIED CRANBERRIES
AND PINOT NOIR

12 medallions of lamb,
   2 to 3 ounces each
3 tablespoons cracked
   peppercorns

Kosher salt
3 tablespoons peanut oil
   (or corn oil)

SAUCE:
3 tablespoons minced shallots
⅓ cup sun-dried cranberries
   (soaked in Pinot Noir
   to soften)
1 cup pinot noir
½ cup demi glace

½ cup strong chicken stock
   (can just use chicken stock)
6 tablespoons unsalted butter
2 tablespoons coarsely
   chopped fresh oregano

Pat lamb medallions dry. Coat evenly with pepper and a good pinch of salt. Lightly pound medallions with meat pounder or heavy saucepan to embed crust of pepper and salt. Set skillet over high heat and lightly coat with oil. When oil begins to smoke, add steaks, a few at a time to not crowd the pan. Sear for 2 to 3 minutes on each side until browned. Meat should be rare. Remove from pan and keep in warm place.

For sauce, pour excess oil from pan. Put pan back on heat. Add shallots and sauté, stir with wooden spoon to bring up dripping, but do not brown. You need to be careful because pan is hot. Add cranberries and heat, stirring to plump slightly. Add wine and reduce by ⅓. Add demi glace and chicken stock and reduce by one-half, until sauce just begins to thicken. Add any juices from lamb and whisk in butter. Place lamb back in the pan, basting for about 1 minute to reheat meat to medium rare. Divide meat evenly onto plates, 2 medallions each. Season sauce with additional cracked pepper and Kosher salt and add oregano. Lightly ladle sauce on meat.

6 servings

COINTREAU CUSTARD TART

MIXX, Pastry Chef/Owner, Kathleen S. Berman

1 11 inch sweet butter crust
   baked to a pale color
3 egg yolks
3 ounces sugar
1½ cups heavy cream

2 tablespoons Cointreau
Blackberries
Raspberries
Apricot glaze

Whisk yolks and sugar by hand until combined. Mix in cream
and Cointreau thoroughly. Strain into pre-baked tart shell. Bake
at 325 degrees until custard is just set. Cool. Chill in refrigerator
until firm. Decorate with fresh blackberries and raspberries.
Brush tart shell edge with apricot glaze.

8 servings

CAFE LOLO, CHEF MICHAEL QUIGLEY

*Warm Flan of Goat Cheese
with Bell Pepper Purée*

*Grilled Day Boat Sea Scallops
with English Peas, Fennel, Corn,
Pearl Onions and Applewood Smoked Bacon
with a Creamy Tarragon Dressing*

*Summer Fruit Shortcakes
with Lemon Curd and Cream*

WARM FLAN OF GOAT CHEESE
WITH BELL PEPPER PURÉE

1 pound goat cheese	½ cup cream reduced to ¼ cup
1 egg	Salt and pepper to taste
2 egg yolks	

Purée first 3 ingredients in food processor until smooth. With motor running, slowly add the cream. Scrape down sides of the bowl, add salt and pepper and turn back on for 10 more seconds until mixed thoroughly. Divide mix into 6 buttered ramekins. Place them in a water bath, cover with foil and bake in a preheated 350 degree oven for about 25-30 minutes. (They are done when inserted with a toothpick and it comes out clean). Invert ramekin onto a plate, lift off ramekin, and spoon the bell pepper purée around the goat cheese. Serve with crusty bread.

BELL PEPPER PURÉE:

3 red bell peppers	Salt and pepper to taste
1 ounce extra virgin olive oil	

Cut peppers in half and remove seeds. Place cut side down in a large sauté pan filled with 2 inches of boiling water and cover. Steam until soft, about 15 minutes. Let peppers cool and purée in blender and add the olive oil and salt and pepper. Strain through a medium strainer and try to push through as many solids as possible. Refrigerate until needed, can be made 1 day ahead.

GRILLED DAY BOAT SEA SCALLOPS WITH ENGLISH PEAS, FENNEL, CORN, PEARL ONIONS AND APPLEWOOD SMOKED BACON WITH A CREAMY TARRAGON DRESSING

18 fresh sea scallops
¾ cup cooked fresh peas
¾ cup cooked shucked corn
¾ cup small diced fennel
¾ cup peeled and roasted pearl onions
¾ cup chopped, cooked Applewood smoked bacon

Tarragon dressing (recipe follows; reserve 6 tablespoons to drizzle over scallops)
6 sprigs Italian parsley
Salt and pepper to taste

In a bowl toss together peas, corn, pearl onions, fennel and bacon. Add salt, pepper, tarragon dressing, and let stand. Season scallops with salt and pepper and grill on a hot grill for about 2 minutes on each side. Remove from heat. Place a neat pile of vegetable mixture in the center of the plate. Place 3 scallops evenly around the vegetable mixture. Drizzle a small amount of tarragon dressing over the scallops, garnish with Italian parsley and serve.

CREAMY TARRAGON DRESSING:

3 egg yolks
Juice of one lemon
1 clove garlic, chopped
2 bunches tarragon, chopped

1½ cups olive oil
1½ cups buttermilk
Salt and pepper to taste

Place first four ingredients in bowl of food processor and buzz for 30 seconds. Then with the machine running, slowly add oil, the buttermilk and salt and pepper. If the dressing is still too thick add a little more buttermilk.

Yield: Serves 6.

SUMMER FRUIT SHORTCAKES
WITH LEMON CURD AND CREAM

6 shortcakes split (recipe
   follows)
1 cup lemon curd (recipe
   follows)

½ cup whipped cream
6 cups assorted, sliced
   seasonal fruits
4 tablespoons sugar

Place fruit in mixing bowl and toss with sugar. Let stand for 20 minutes. Place bottom half of shortcake on serving plate and spoon equal amounts of fruit over shortcake bottom. Drizzle each with lemon curd and put a dollop of whipped cream over each. Place top half of shortcake on top at an angle. Dust plate with powdered sugar and serve.

SHORTCAKE:
2 cups flour
1 tablespoon baking powder
½ teaspoon salt
⅓ cup sugar

½ cup butter
1 egg
1 cup cream

Mix flour, baking powder, salt, sugar and butter. Add egg and cream. Roll and cut. Brush tops with melted butter and sprinkle with sugar. Bake at 350 degrees for 10-12 minutes.

LEMON CURD:
3½ tablespoons lemon zest
1¾ cups lemon juice
12 beaten eggs

2½ cups sugar
1¼ cups melted butter

Combine all ingredients and cook on top of stove until thick. Strain and cool.

It is not necessary to use a double boiler.

Yield: Serves 6

NAT TATE,
FORMERLY OF
EAST SIDE OYSTER BAR AND GRILL

Semolina Crusted Goat Cheese Croquette

*Mixed Summer Greens Tossed
with Meyer Lemon Vinaigrette,
Baby Artichokes, Roasted Garlic,
Bacon and Daikon Threads*

*Shrimp Encrusted Sea Bass
on a Pedestal of Basmati-Lentil Pilaf,
Surrounded by a Warm Salad of Organic Beets,
Yellow Wax and Blue Lake Beans
with Aged Sherry Vinaigrette and Sweet herbs*

Peach-Lavender Ice Cream

SEMOLINA CRUSTED
GOAT CHEESE CROQUETTE

CROQUETTE:

3 ounce patty of goat cheese - chevre

Buttermilk

Semolina/flour mix (70%/30%)

Peanut oil for deep frying

Dredge goat cheese patty in buttermilk and semolina mix. Deep fry in peanut oil. Set aside.

VINAIGRETTE:

1 ounce Meyer lemon juice

1 ounce Champagne vinegar

1 ounce extra virgin olive oil

3 ounces pure olive oil

pinch toasted mustard seeds

pinch toasted and ground coriander seeds

Salt and black pepper to taste

Reserve vinaigrette for later use, keeps well.

SALAD:

2-3 baby artichokes, blanched, half-way peeled and quartered

5-6 cloves of roasted garlic

1 slice crispy julienne strips of applewood smoked bacon

Fresh organic mixed greens

Spun daikon threads

Use a vegetable "spinner" (found in gourmet stores or Chinatown) to make the spun daikon threads

To assemble:

Toss the greens in the vinaigrette, make a nice high mound in the center of the plate, quarter the artichokes and place around the greens, sprinkle the roasted garlic cloves around. Do the same with the bacon. Put the daikon threads on top of greens. Lean the finished "croquette" on the side of the greens

1 tart, increase for number of tarts desired

SHRIMP ENCRUSTED SEA BASS

¾ cup rock shrimp
1 teaspoon chopped ginger
1 teaspoon chopped garlic
1 teaspoon chopped jalapeno
   pepper

1 egg white
Salt and white pepper to taste
pinch cumin seeds, toasted
   and ground
6 sea bass filets

Place all ingredients in a food processor and pulse until incorpo-rated. Don't over pulse, it will overwork the proteins in the rock shrimp and become rubbery when cooked. Paste rock shrimp farce on the top side of the sea bass filets, set aside.

Pan sear fish with rock shrimp side down first. When golden brown flip them over to finish into 350 degree oven for 3 to 5 minutes. Don't overcook.

6 servings

BASMATI-LENTIL PILAF

½ cup diced onions
1 tablespoon diced shallots
½ tablespoon chopped garlic
¼ cup diced red pepper
½ cup red lentils
1 cup Basmati rice

½ cup white wine
2 cups chicken stock
Salt and black pepper to taste
2 tablespoons scallions,
   bias cut
2 ounces olive oil

Sweat onions, shallots, garlic together. No color. Add salt and pepper. Add lentils and cook out for 3 to 4 minutes. Add basmati and cook out for 1 to 2 minutes. Deglaze with wine, add peppers and stock. Bring to a boil, reduce to a simmer and cook for approximately 18 minutes. Add scallions after it is cooked.

6 servings

BEET AND BEAN SALAD

VINAIGRETTE:

1 ounce aged Sherry
1 ounce Sherry vinegar
½ ounce lemon juice
pinch chili flakes

Salt and pepper to taste
3 ounces pure olive oil
1 ounce extra virgin olive oil

SALAD:

6 medium red beets
8 ounces Blue Lake green
   beans

8 ounces yellow wax beans
¼ cup sweet herbs, tarragon,
   basil, chervil, dill, parsley

Blanch and shock yellow wax beans and Blue Lake green beans. Boil the beets until tender, peel and cut into 6 or 8 wedges depending on size of beets. Slice sweet herbs. Put 2 ounces of vinaigrette (per person), beans, beets and sweet herbs in a stainless mixing bowl over a boiling pot of water and warm gently.

To assemble: Use 12 inch plate, place a 4 inch PVC pipe or ring mold in the center of the plate. Bind warm pilaf with a little butter and pack ½ to ¾ cup of it into mold, tamp down with a squeeze bottle or something similar. Remove mold. Surround pilaf with warm beet and bean salad. Place sea bass (rock shrimp side up) on top of pilaf. Place crispy fried julienne leeks on top of sea bass for garnish and texture.

PEACH-LAVENDER ICE CREAM

2 cups whole milk
½ cup honey
1 teaspoon dried lavender
   blossom
1 teaspoon Meyer lemon zest
6 egg yolks

½ cup sugar
dash salt
2 cups heavy cream
2 tablespoons lemon juice
1 teaspoon vanilla extract
2 large peaches, ripe, diced

Simmer milk, honey, zest and lavender until honey is melted. Steep 30 minutes, strain. Whisk yolks, sugar and salt for 3 to 4 minutes until pale yellow. Gradually whisk in milk mixture. Cook over double boiler for 8 to 10 minutes (not too hot). It is done when the custard coats the back of a spoon. Stir in cream, lemon juice and vanilla and peaches. Chill and then pour into an ice cream machine and freeze accordingly.

CHEF BRIAN O'NEAL,
FORMERLY HEAD CHEF,
SOUTHSIDE SALOON AND DINING HALL

*These recipes work well both individually or collectively, making a
wonderful meal.*

First course:
Fresh shucked oysters with a
green tomatillo cocktail sauce.

Second Course:
A light Eggplant Lasagna using fresh vegetables that can
be grown in your own back yard, including balsamic red
onions, oven roasted tomatoes, and grilled zucchini all
served with a tomato coulis and hummus.

Third course and main plate:
One of my favorite dishes is a lightly smoked thick cut
pork chop, grilled and finished in the oven and served
with a chayote salsa and smoked corn polenta finished
with a touch of chili oil and fresh chopped cilantro.

Fourth course, dessert:
In my opinion dessert is one of the most important items
on the menu. This is because it is the last thing people
eat. If it is good, it makes the rest of the food look great
and if it is bad...well, you know. The dessert I want to
share is one of my favorites. It includes a multitude of
different foods from Sonoma County; Gravenstein
apples, dried persimmons, and butter.

FRESH SHUCKED OYSTERS

Shuck oyster and put a small teaspoon amount of Green Tomatillo Cocktail Sauce on oyster before eating (recipe follows). If
you don't know how to shuck an oyster most seafood depart-
ments at grocery stores will take the time to show you.

GREEN TOMATILLO COCKTAIL SAUCE

½ medium onion, rough chop
3 tablespoons chopped
  cilantro stems
1 teaspoon minced ginger
1 pound tomatillos, peeled
2-3 serranos
⅛ cup olive oil

¼ cup parsley leaves blanched
  in salted water for 10-15
  seconds, then shocked in
  cold water and squeezed dry
4-5 large mint leaves
1 lime

Roast (with no oil) tomatillo and serranos with salt and pepper
in 400 degree oven, tossing occasionally until they are cooked
½ way through. Cooking time in the oven is about 10 minutes.
Place on sheet pan and let cool in refrigerator. Saute until
translucent the onion, cilantro stems and ginger. Let cool. Puree
tomatillo mixture and onion mixture in blender and transfer to
mixing bowl. In blender put 4 - 5 large mint leaves and parsley,
turn on and drizzle olive oil until homogeneous (a thick tex-
tured puree). Add parsley, mint oil and the juice of one lime to
tomatillo mixture. Incorporate thoroughly and season to taste.

HUMMUS

1 pound cooked garbanzo
  beans
1 tablespoon finely mined
  garlic
¼ cup olive oil
2 tablespoons lemon juice

3 tablespoons sesame tahini
2 teaspoons cumin seed,
  toasted and ground
Pinch cayenne
Salt and black pepper to taste

Puree beans in food processor until smooth. Remove and place
in a large mixing bowl. With a whisk, mix in remaining ingredients and adjust seasoning as necessary.

LASAGNA

Eggplant	Salt and pepper
Zucchini	Balsamic vinegar
Roma tomatoes	Red wine vinegar
Red onions	Goat cheese (chevre)
Olive oil	Soft Jack cheese

To cook vegetables for lasagna:

Eggplant: Cut eggplant into rounds and ¼ to ⅔ inch thick. Three slices gives you one dish. Lightly oil and season with salt and pepper and grill until softened.

Zucchini: Cut zucchini on an angle and cook to the same specifications as the eggplant. Three slices is enough for one dish.

Tomatoes: Cut tomatoes in half lengthwise and lay on sheet pan, round side down. Season with red wine vinegar, dry oregano, salt and pepper. Roast in oven until soft, approximately 45 minutes at 375 degrees. One tomato is enough to one dish.

Onions: Slice ends off onion and peel dry skin. Slice ½ inch thick rounds and lay on sheet pan. Drizzle both balsamic vinegar and olive oil on both sides of onion as well as seasoning to taste with salt and black pepper. Allow onions to marinade for about 30 minutes at room temperature. Then roast in 350 degree oven for 1 to 1½ hours, flipping onions about every 30 minutes. One slice is enough for one dish.

TO PLATE THE EGGPLANT LASAGNA:
First make sure all vegetables and coulis are hot to the touch. Ladle approximately 2 ounces of tomato coulis onto center of plate. In the middle of the tomato coulis, lay one balsamic onion round. Top that with one grilled eggplant round. Then one slice of Jack cheese. Place two halves of tomatoes round side down on top of the cheese. Top the tomatoes with another round of grilled eggplant. The next layer use the grilled zucchini. Cover the zucchini with the third piece of grilled eggplant. Crumble the goat cheese over the top and slide the whole tower into the oven and remove once cheese has warmed. Place one spoonful of hummus on side of plate and serve with a couple of bread crisps. Finish with a sprinkle of fresh chopped parsley for color if you like.

TOMATO COULIS

1 pound roma tomatoes vine
   ripened, rough chop
6 ounces white onion,
   medium chop
3 ounces carrot, small chop
3 ounces celery, small chop
1 bay leaf

1 teaspoon chili flakes
1 tablespoon fresh picked
   thyme
¼ cup red cooking wine
½-1 cup chicken broth
   (depending on how juicy
   your tomatoes are)

Saute onion, carrot, celery, bay leaf, chili flakes, and thyme in a
heavy bottom sauce pan. Saute until onions are translucent,
then deglaze with red wine and stir. Add chopped tomatoes and
chicken broth and allow to simmer for 30 minutes. Once
cooked, puree in blender until smooth and push through a
double mesh strainer.

GRILLED PORK CHOP

1 12 ounce pork chop

¼ cup pork cure
   (recipe follows)

Rub the chop on all sides and let rest for 30 minutes.

TO SMOKE:
You can use any barbeque by placing a few coals at the bottom
to one side and light them. Once coals have a red glow cover
with mesquite or hickory wood chips that have been soaked in
water (you can find these chips at most local shopping markets),
place cured pork chop on grill on the opposite side as the wood
coals. Cover with a lid and allow to smoke for 15 minutes.

PORK CURE

1 cup sugar, granulated
½ cup salt, kosher
½ orange, zest
¼ bunch sage, minced
1½ garlic cloves, minced

1 tablespoon juniper berries
   lightly toasted and ground
½ tablespoon chili flakes
1 teaspoon ground cardamom

Mix well and store in an air tight container.

SMOKED CORN SOFT POLENTA

2½ cups chicken stock
2½ cups manufacturing cream
  (heavy cream)
½ cup semolina flour

½ cup polenta
¼ cup dry Jack cheese (grated)
1 cup smoked corn kernels
Salt and white pepper to taste

In a heavy bottom saucepan, heat chicken stock and cream to a simmer. Add semolina and polenta, stirring to incorporate. Allow to cook for 15 minutes on a low heat, stirring occasionally to keep from sticking to bottom. Once the polenta begins to pull away from the sides while stirring it is done. Remove from heat and add cheese, corn and seasonings. To smoke the kernels of corn, place a couple of ears of corn in the smoker at the same time you do the pork. Then simply cut the kernels off the ear and add them to your polenta.

TO COOK AND PLATE THE PORK CHOP:
Fire up the grill and cook the pork chop long enough to get nice grill marks and the great grill flavor. Finish in a 350 degree oven for 20 minutes. Make sure the chayote salsa and polenta are warm (you may need to add a touch of cream to reheat the polenta). Place a large spoonful of polenta at the top of your plate. Use the spoon to make a crater in the center of the polenta and fill it with the warm chayote salsa. Lean the cooked pork chop against the polenta and finish the dish with chopped cilantro and ancho chili oil drizzle.

CHAYOTE SALSA

2 chayote squash
1½ pounds tomatillo, peeled
1 red bell pepper
1 yellow bell pepper
1 jalapeno pepper
½ large red onion

1 ounce lime juice
½ bunch picked cilantro
  leaves
¼ tablespoon cumin seeds
  (toast and grind)
Salt and black pepper to taste

Slice the squash about ¼ inch thick. Toss in ¼ cup olive oil and grill until lightly charred. Cut squash into ¼ inch dice and place in bowl. Roast bell peppers, remove seeds and peel. Cut peppers into small dice and add to bowl. Slice onion ¼ inch thick, oil, salt, pepper and grill until broken down. Dice onion and add to bowl. Roast tomatillo and jalapeno in oven until soft. Remove stems and seeds from the jalapeno. Puree tomatillo and jalapenos and add to bowl. Add all other ingredients and season to taste.

ANCHO CHILI OIL

5 ancho chili pods
3 sundried tomatoes
3 cloves of peeled garlic

1 tablespoon chili flakes
2 quarts olive oil

Reconstitute dry peppers in water. Once peppers are soft, remove from water, pat dry and add to oil with all other ingredients. Bring oil up to temperature (approximately 140° F.), then reduce heat to as low as possible. Cook for 30 minutes. Puree all ingredients in blender and then let sit aside and settle. Best if done the day before. The oil that floats is the chili oil that you want to use.

APPLE AND PERSIMMON TARTE TATIN

8 Gravenstein apples
6-8 dry persimmon slices
¾ cup sugar
1 teaspoon lemon juice
1 teaspoon cinnamon

1 teaspoon powdered ginger
4 tablespoons butter
Sweet pastry dough (recipe follows)

Reconstitute dry persimmon in water. Warm on stove until soft. Peel, core and halve the apples. In a 10 inch saute pan combine sugar, lemon juice, cinnamon, ginger powder and a touch of water. Bring to a boil stirring to dissolve the sugar. Stop stirring and let the boil caramelize the sugar until golden brown. Remove from heat. Stir in butter until melted. Lay the apples in the sauté pan with the inside halves facing up. Pack tightly and create a second layer if needed. Place a layer of persimmons on top of the apples. Return to heat and allow apples and persimmons to cook, cover with a lid. When soft, uncover and continue to cook until the sauce reduces to a glaze. Roll out sweet pastry dough and slide over the top of the sauté pan. Cut off any excess dough. Season by brushing pastry dough with egg wash and sprinkle with cinnamon and sugar. Return sauté pan to 350 degree oven and finish cooking until pastry is golden brown. Takes about 20 minutes. Cool slightly and invert on a platter. Serve with a scoop of ice cream. Egg wash consists of: 1 egg, 1 tablespoon water, 1 teaspoon salt and 1 teaspoon sugar. Whip to combine.

SWEET PASTRY DOUGH

1 cup all purpose flour
⅔ cup sugar
pinch salt
¼ teaspoon baking powder

4 tablespoons butter, cold as
   possible
1 egg

Mix together dry ingredients and cut in butter. Whip egg to break up and mix it in the flour-butter mixture. Press together and wrap in plastic. Let chill in refrigerator until needed.

MISTRAL RESTAURANT, PROPRIETOR MICHAEL HIRSCHBERG; CHEF, SHEILA PARROTT

—A Tasting Dinner—

Standup Hors d'oeuvres

1994 Sonoma Cutrer Chardonnay

Roast Monkfish in Red Wine Sauce

1994 De Loach Pinot Noir O.F.S.

Little Salad of Summer Greens

Roast Leg of Sonoma County Lamb

*with Wild Mushroom Ravioli
and a Confit of Roast Vegetables*

1992 Stonestreet Cabernet Sauvignon

Italian Baked Vanilla Cream

Kahlua-Caramel Sauce

ROAST MONKFISH IN RED WINE SAUCE

1½ pounds monkfish tail
¼ teaspoon whole black
  peppercorns, crushed
½ teaspoon chopped fresh
  thyme leaves
¼ cup minced shallots

2 tablespoons olive oil
1 teaspoon salt
⅔ cup red wine
¾ cup butter, chilled and cut
  in small pieces

Trim monkfish and portion in 3 ounce pieces. Marinate with peppercorns, thyme, one tablespoon olive oil and one table-spoon minced shallots. Leave for several hours in refrigerator. Prepare sauce by reducing red wine with rest of minced shallots until syrupy. Remove from heat and whisk in butter a little bit at a time until thickened. Hold in a warm place away from direct heat or sauce will break.

Remove monkfish from marinade and wipe dry. Season with salt. In a sauté pan with remaining olive oil, over medium high heat, brown fish on all sides. Place in 400 degree oven until cooked through. Time will depend on thickness of fish. Remove from oven and let rest for 5 minutes. Slice each portion into three pieces across the grain and arrange on warm plates each covered with a pool of red wine sauce. Serve.

Serves 4 as an appetizer

ROAST LEG OF LAMB

1 leg of lamb, hip bone removed

Season lamb with chopped garlic, chopped rosemary (or other herb), salt and pepper. Roll and tie the leg for roasting. Roast at 450 degrees until internal temperature reaches 140 degrees.

WILD MUSHROOM RAVIOLI

PASTA:
¾ pound semolina
½ pound flour
4 eggs

1 ounce oil
¼ cup water (or less)

Combine flours. Combine liquids. Mix together. Form into dough ball. Knead until smooth.

WILD MUSHROOM FILLING:
2 pounds assorted wild
   mushrooms, chopped
½ cup minced shallots

1 bunch parsley, chopped fine
½ cup ricotta

Saute shallots in light olive oil until transparent. Add mushrooms and continue sauteing until wilted. Season with parsley, salt and pepper. Allow to cool. When cool, bind with ricotta. Chill until ready to form ravioli.

To assemble ravioli: Divide pasta dough in half. Roll out one half (by hand or machine) into a long rectangle of uniform thinness. Form filling into balls of desired size and place them evenly atop the pasta sheet. Roll out the second half of pasta into a shape closely resembling the first. Spray mist the pasta sheets on the sides that will meet. Place the second sheet atop the first and press the dough around the balls of filling. Crimp cut between the ravioli using a pasta wheel. If not to be used right away, dust the ravioli with flour to keep them from sticking.

To cook ravioli: Bring a large volume of water to the boil. Add salt. Plunge ravioli into boiling water. Cook approximately 2 minutes until edges of ravioli are tender but still "al dente".

ROAST VEGETABLE CONFIT

1 eggplant
4 bell peppers
3 red onions

2 heads of garlic
4 zucchini or summer squash
1 pound red potatoes

Keeping each vegetable separate, prepare them as follows:
Eggplant - cut into large 2 inch cubes

Peppers - remove top and seeds, cut into 6 or 8 squares

Onions - peel and cut in quarters (eighths if large torpedo type)

Garlic - peel and divide into whole cloves

Squash - cut into 2 inch cubes or rounds

Potatoes - cut into 2 inch cubes

Each vegetable must be roasted individually before combining!

Place each vegetable in a separate bowl. Drizzle each with virgin olive oil and toss so as to lightly coat them. Place vegetable on a baking sheet and roast at 450 degrees until just tender.

Let each vegetable cool. Gently combine all vegetables and season with salt and pepper.

To serve: Spread mixture on a baking sheet and roast in a 450 degree oven until warm.

ITALIAN BAKED VANILLA CREAM

12 egg yolks
1¼ cup sugar
6 cups cream

1 vanilla bean, split
pinch salt

Heat cream to boiling with vanilla bean and salt. Scrape bean seeds into cream. Combine yolks and sugar, slowly pour in cream and mix gently. Divide into buttered ramekins. Bake in water bath, covered at 350 degrees until set, about 45 minutes. Cool and refrigerate.

KAHLUA - CARAMEL SAUCE

2 cups water
8 cups sugar
5 cups hot water

1 cup kahlua
1 cup espresso

Mix water and sugar together. Caramelize. Slowly add hot water to dissolve caramel. Remove from heat and add kahlua. Add espresso. Sauce should be a light syrup.

Chef Bernadette Burrell,
Dempsey's Sonoma Brewing Company

The following is a complete autumn dinner to serve four guests. Sonoma County is home to many small purveyors of quality ingredients. You can shop in local markets and look for Select Sonoma County ingredients. Be creative and have fun cooking.

Carrot Ginger Soup

Spinach Salad with Sherry Vinaigrette

Corn and Chile Salsa

Roasted Rabbit with Root Vegetables

Apple Pear Crisp with Crumb Topping

CARROT GINGER SOUP

3 tablespoons olive oil
2 onions, chopped
2 tablespoons grated fresh
  ginger
1 cup white wine
2 pears, peeled and chopped
5 cups carrots, peeled and
  chopped

6 cups chicken stock
2 tablespoons sugar
Salt and pepper to taste
1 teaspoon cumin
1 teaspoon coriander
½ cup heavy cream (or half
  and half or none)
Chopped cilantro for garnish

Saute onions until translucent. Add ginger, pears and carrots.
Continue to saute for five minutes. Add white wine and reduce
by half. Add chicken stock. Bring to a boil and reduce to a
simmer until carrots are tender. Puree the soup in a blender.
Return to a sauce pan and add the salt, pepper, sugar, optional
cream, cumin and coriander. Garnish the soup with chopped
cilantro.

SPINACH SALAD

1 pound loose spinach
  (farmer's markets offer
  interesting varieties)
4 fresh beets roasted until
  tender and sliced
1 cup roasted walnuts

2 apples thinly sliced
  (Gravenstein, Fuji, Granny
  Smith)
8 ounces goat cheese
Sherry Vinaigrette (recipe
  follows)

Wash spinach and dry thoroughly. Place in a large bowl. Add
beets, walnuts, apples and goat cheese. Gently toss until well
incorporated. Slowly add dressing. Toss greens until lightly
coated. You may adjust amount of dressing on salad according to
your personal taste.

SHERRY VINAIGRETTE:
10 tablespoons olive oil
4 tablespoons sherry vinegar

Salt and pepper to taste
3 shallots finely diced

Place olive oil in a bowl. Pour vinegar in a slow steady stream
into the olive oil. Add salt and pepper to taste. Add shallots.

CORN AND CHILE SALSA

4 ears of corn husked, washed and kernels removed
4 scallions thinly sliced
2 tablespoons minced chipotle peppers
2 limes juiced

2 tablespoons apple cider vinegar
6 tablespoons olive oil
1 teaspoon minced garlic
2 teaspoons sugar

In a large bowl mix the corn kernels with all the remaining ingredients. This salsa will keep for three or four days.

ROASTED RABBIT
WITH ROASTED ROOT VEGETABLES

ROASTED RABBIT:
1 whole rabbit, cut into six pieces
2 cloves garlic, peeled and chopped
2 cups amber style beer

2 tablespoons achiote paste (found in Mexican grocery stores)
Salt and pepper
2 tablespoons olive oil

Mix garlic, beer, achiote paste, salt, pepper and olive oil in a bowl and thoroughly combine. Place rabbit into marinade and cover. Refrigerate for 24 hours.

Bring rabbit to room temperature. Heat a grill or broiler. Remove rabbit from the marinade. Brush with the marinade and grill or broil turning occasionally, until cooked through, about 15 minutes.

ROASTED ROOT VEGETABLES:
Go to your favorite grocery store or farmer's market and pick out two pieces of six different varieties of root vegetables. For example, yams, rutabagas, turnips, parsnips, sweet potatoes. Preheat oven to 350 degrees.

Peel and dice all vegetables about one inch in diameter. Toss with olive oil, salt and pepper and one teaspoon of your favorite herb. Thyme is a good one. Place vegetables on a sheet pan and roast in the oven on the top shelf until tender but not mushy. Serve along side the rabbit.

APPLE PEAR CRISP

CRISP:

2½ pounds apples
2½ pounds pears
¼ cup brown sugar
¼ teaspoon nutmeg
¼ teaspoon cinnamon

2 lemons, juice and zest
1 vanilla bean, scraped
Crumb topping (recipe
   follows)

Preheat oven to 350 degrees. Dice apples and pears. It is not necessary to peel them. Place in a bowl and toss with other ingredients. Place in a baking dish and put ½ inch of crumb topping on top. Bake for 45 minutes or until the crisp begins to bubble and turn golden brown.

CRUMB TOPPING:

1 cup flour
½ cup brown sugar
¼ teaspoon salt

4 ounces butter
1 cup walnuts, toasted

Place flour, brown sugar and salt in a bowl. Work in the butter with your fingers or an electric mixer, mixing until the topping is crumbly and begins to hold together. Add the nuts and quickly mix them in.

PARTICIPATING RESTAURANTS

Chefs of restaurants, wineries and food producers have made the publication of this book possible. Following is a list of participating restaurants.

Aram's Café, Bruce Osterlye, Petaluma
Bear Flag Café, Gerald Lowe, Sonoma
Bistro Ralph, Ralph Tingle, Healdsburg
Buona Sera, Sandy Poze, Petaluma,
Café Buon Gusto, James D'Ottavio, Santa Rosa
Café Citti, Luca Citti, Kenwood
Café Europe, Robert Buchshachermaier, Santa Rosa
Café Lolo, Michael Quigley, Santa Rosa
Café Portofino, Maria Belmonte, Santa Rosa
Center City Diner, Michael Valmossoi, Petaluma
Depot Hotel, Michael Ghilarducci, Sonoma
Della Santina's, Dan Della Santina, Sonoma
Dempsey's, Bernadette Burrell, Petaluma
De Schmire, Robert Steiner, Petaluma
Fino's Cucina Italiana, Franco Leicata and Ferruccilo Morrasi, Petaluma
Glen Ellen Inn Restaurant, Christian Bernard, Glen Ellen
Graziano's Ristorante, Graziano Perozzi, Petaluma
Healdsburg Charcuterie, Patrick Martin, Healdsburg
Inn at the Tides, Carlo Galazzo, Bodega Bay
John Ash & Co., Jeffrey Madura, Santa Rosa
Kenwood Restaurant and Bar, Max Schacher, Kenwood
Le Bistro, Corey Basso, Petaluma
Lisa Hemenway, Lisa Hemenway, Santa Rosa
Madrona Manor, Todd Muir, Healdsburg
Mistral, Sheilah Parrott, Santa Rosa
MIXX, Dan Berman and Kathleen Berman, Santa Rosa
Catelli's The Rex, Randy Hoppe, Geyserville
River House, Greg Tully, Petaluma
J. M. Rosen's Waterfront Grill, Jan Rosen, Petaluma
Topolos Russian River Vineyards Restaurant, Bob Engel, Forestville
The Café, Sonoma Mission Inn & Spa, Philip Breitweiser,
    Boyes Hot Springs
The Grille, Sonoma Mission Inn & Spa, Tony Sakaguchi,
    Boyes Hot Springs

For more information about our winery and food producer contributors, please see the co-sponsor articles featured throughout the cookbook.

SONOMA COUNTY
PARTICIPATING WINERIES

Alexander Valley Vineyards
Armida Winery
Arrowood Vineyards and Winery
Chateau St. Jean
Chateau Souverain
Cline Cellars
De Loach Vineyards
Glen Ellen Winery
Gloria Ferrer Champagne Cellars
J Wine Company
Jordan Vineyard and Winery
Kendall-Jackson Winery
Kenwood Vineyards
Korbel Champagne Cellars
La Crema Winery
Matanzas Creek Winery
Murphy-Goode Winery
Paradise Ridge Winery
Pedroncelli Winery
Simi Winery
Topolos Russian River Vineyards
Viansa Winery
Windsor Vineyard

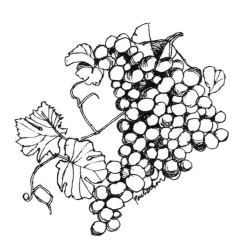

A

M

N

O

P

Tip Clo through your two lips.

Splendor
in the glass

Sonoma County – Its Bounty
64 Jessie Lane, Petaluma, CA 94952

Please send _____ copies of SONOMA COUNTY – ITS BOUNTY · · · · · $19.95 each _____
 California residents add 7.5% sales tax · · · · · · · · · · · · · · · · · $ 1.50 each _____
 Postage and handling · $ 3.00 each _____
 Total Enclosed _____

Name _____

Address _____

City _____State _____ Zip _____
_____ Check or money order enclosed
_____ Visa / Mastercard No. _____Exp. Date _____

Signature _____
Make checks payable to Clover Stornetta Farms. Profits will directly benefit the Sonoma County
Agricultural Fund c/o Sonoma County Community Foundation.

– –

Sonoma County – Its Bounty
64 Jessie Lane, Petaluma, CA 94952

Please send _____ copies of SONOMA COUNTY – ITS BOUNTY · · · · · $19.95 each _____
 California residents add 7.5% sales tax · · · · · · · · · · · · · · · · · $ 1.50 each _____
 Postage and handling · $ 3.00 each _____
 Total Enclosed _____

Name _____

Address _____

City _____State _____ Zip _____
_____ Check or money order enclosed
_____ Visa / Mastercard No. _____Exp. Date _____

Signature _____
Make checks payable to Clover Stornetta Farms. Profits will directly benefit the Sonoma County
Agricultural Fund c/o Sonoma County Community Foundation.

– –

Sonoma County – Its Bounty
64 Jessie Lane, Petaluma, CA 94952

Please send _____ copies of SONOMA COUNTY – ITS BOUNTY · · · · · $19.95 each _____
 California residents add 7.5% sales tax · · · · · · · · · · · · · · · · · $ 1.50 each _____
 Postage and handling · $ 3.00 each _____
 Total Enclosed _____

Name _____

Address _____

City _____State _____ Zip _____
_____ Check or money order enclosed
_____ Visa / Mastercard No. _____Exp. Date _____

Signature _____
Make checks payable to Clover Stornetta Farms. Profits will directly benefit the Sonoma County
Agricultural Fund c/o Sonoma County Community Foundation.